ILLUSION

JR

RETHINKING SUCCESS IN THE LIGHT OF THE STORY OF JOSEPH

ILLUSIONS OF GRANDEUR

RETHINKING SUCCESS IN THE LIGHT OF THE STORY OF JOSEPH

Vicky Calver

Scripture Union, 207-209 Queensway, Bletchley, MK2 2EB, England, UK
Email: info@scriptureunion.org.uk
Website: www.scriptureunion.org.uk

ISBN: 1 84427 168 4

Scripture Union Australia
Locked Bag 2, Central Coast Business Centre, NSW 2252
www.su.org.au

Scripture Union USA
PO Box 987#1
Valley Forge
PA 19482, USA
www.scriptureunion.org

First published in the U.K. by Scripture Union, 2006

British Library Cataloguing-in-Publication data
A catalogue record for this book is available from the British Library.
Cover design: ie design
Internal design and typesetting by Creative Pages
Printed in Great Britain by Creative Print and Design, Ebbw Vale, Wales

Scripture Union is an international Christian charity working with churches in more than 130 countries, providing resources to bring the good news about Jesus Christ to children, young people and families and to encourage them to develop spiritually through the Bible and prayer. As well as coordinating our network of volunteers, staff and associates who run holidays, church-based events and school Christian groups, we produce a wide range of publications and support those who use our resources through training programmes.

To Don and Madge Ford

On behalf of the many in the UK and overseas
whom you have walked beside, and who have
tried to learn from your example what it is
to live without illusions of grandeur

What others think of
Illusions of Grandeur

'I love this book! Vicky Calver's unadulterated honesty, together with a passionate desire to know God's will, is no more evident than within the pages of *Illusions of Grandeur*. Vicky challenges us to look within at our personal motivation and desire for success. She draws powerful and often moving anecdotal parallels between her own remarkable journey and that of the story of Joseph. She left me in no doubt about the relevance of this Old Testament "dreamer" to our twenty-first century lives. *Illusions of Grandeur* may well change your thoughts on "successful" living forever!'

Diane Louise Jordan, TV Presenter and Speaker

'Vicky in her eloquent and real way challenges the search for significance, evaluates the pursuit of purpose and asks in a provocative way, "What is it that really drives us?" I feel this book will facilitate a fruitful journey to answering those deeper questions about why we want to succeed and who we are really trying to please while pointing to what really matters. A refreshing, honest, fun and thoughtful read – enjoy.'

Finlay Wood, ex-bouncer, currently working as a builder and counsellor.

'We live in a world that has a strange and warped view of success, a world that has a preoccupation with possessions, position and power. This book, packed with personal examples and refreshing honesty, paints a very helpful picture as to what true success might look like – success which is born out of a greater understanding of why we are here and what we are here to do.'

Jim Partridge, Head of Youth and Student Ministry, Spring Harvest

'Vicky Calver weaves the intriguing story of Joseph with her own story – and with ours – to help us dream the best dreams for our lives. We may be enticed by any number of dreams – of grandeur, leisure, fame, power, pleasure, security as success – but none of them will satisfy. Vicky points us to a better dream by far.'

Brian and Grace McLaren are involved in pastoral ministry and with the Emergent network (emergentvillage.com).

'This book provides a refreshingly real perspective on the definition of success in Christian terms and how it is often distorted – both by the world and the church. As a youth worker, this book reminds me not to shy away from the realities of suffering or weakness (my own and others') and to appreciate the individuality of each young person in my charge. I believe it also conveys a vital message for all in Christian leadership about the issues and internal conflicts of this generation ... read it!'

Claire Richardson, youth worker

'Vicky's approach to the story of Joseph is very insightful, picking up the fact that Joseph was ingenuous in nature, and recognised that he paid more attention to significance rather than success in God's purposes. Particularly with our success-driven culture this is a refreshing and provocative book, with a very real, personal, human touch.'

Roy Crowne, National Director, Youth for Christ

'This is an endearing and captivating account of a personal journey which uses the story of Joseph as a biblical mirror. A really good read.'

Joel Edwards, General Director, Evangelical Alliance

Contents

Acknowledgements

A book may have one author, but many people are involved in bringing it into being. This is no exception. I am indebted to more people than I can name. To each and every person who helped shape my thinking and gave input into this book – thank you.

I am grateful to those at Scripture Union who saw the need for such a book and were willing to publish it. I particularly appreciate the support of my editors: Andrew Cupples helped me start the process; and Andrew Clark has seen me through it.

Over the years, I have been challenged by the example and ministry of the band, Delirious?. Their passion to go deeper in faith and to encourage a generation to make a difference is something I share. Therefore, I am deeply honoured and grateful that Martin Smith agreed to write the foreword for this book.

Thank you to each person who allowed me to share their story. I want to say how much I appreciate your honesty, vulnerability and example. I would also like to thank Coreene, Chris and Sarah, Helen, Gavin and Dad who gave input on the draft manuscript. Your insights have brought depth to the text and your involvement has been a real encouragement to me.

I am not a hermit when I write. I am grateful to all the friends who allowed their brains to be picked, to those that gave feedback on different chapters and to all the strangers in random coffee shops and other places who shared their thoughts and ideas with me!

As much as I have commented on the challenges of being a leader's kid, I want to say how much I value my parents' example. They not only talked about what it means to follow Jesus wherever he takes you – they lived it. Thank you for being such a significant part of my life, despite the miles. Thank you also to my siblings: Kris, Gavin, and Suzy, and to my sister-in-law, Anne. I really appreciate all your friendship, encouragement and support. Thank you for your parts in this ongoing story.

I want to thank my grandparents for the ways that they have demonstrated what it means to grow in faith, even when life gets limited. And to PJ and Ingrid, my aunt and uncle, who gave me a home when I needed it most.

I am also grateful to my flatmates for putting up with an author in the house! Thank you for rejoicing with me, listening to the challenges and staying up late chatting. Thanks also to the many others who have walked with me through this process. Particularly to Addie for her prayerful insights, and to Kareena and Carolyn for keeping me sane!

I would like to express my thanks to my colleagues at Global Connections for their support and encouragement in this process. I am also grateful to those in Raynes Park Community Church (London) and Walnut Hill Community Church (Connecticut, USA) for their prayers and interest.

Above all, I want to thank God for his faithfulness. My prayer is that this book will help all of us explore what it means to have deeper faith.

Foreword

My earliest memories of church were being taken to a small gospel hall every Sunday. It seems hard to believe now but the men still wore suits and the ladies hats, we knew what songs were coming next as the hymn numbers were put on a board for all to see, and we all sang our hearts out, never fully drowning out the organ that was suspiciously louder than some guitar amps today! God gave me a dream even then to see church music played on the radio so that ordinary people, many who would never step foot in a church, would in some way be exposed to a message of hope and the good news.

Many years on, that dream is still alive and some of the things I imagined have happened. But here's the thing, nothing has gone to plan and there have been many disappointments along with the successes and I've had to learn the hard way that it's about remaining faithful to the God who gave us the dream in the first place. When you have dreams and ambitions in your hand you always imagine how it's going to look and feel. After all God put the dreams there and surely he is gonna see to it that it all happens for his glory. The only snag to this is that we find out that God is more interested in our hearts than our ambitions, even if they are mostly inspired by himself.

The Christian life is often described as a 'race' and we are called to finish it in one piece with dignity and our relationships still intact. Often we discover along the way that love is more powerful than our achievements and that purity in our walk with God is more eternally significant than the medals we earn.

This book is an honest account of the struggle between the call of God and the fact that life doesn't always turn out how we want it. To stay confident in our Creator that his will is perfect because he always knows best. Vicky is a shining example of someone who even through the struggles and disappointments has grasped the 'bigger' picture and been faithful in the small. She will see her God do extraordinary things in her lifetime. Read it, dream it and finish well.

Martin Smith, Lead vocalist of Delirious?

Boxes are for things, not for people
So don't try to limit me to fit your image
Or label me according to your standards
I want no illusions of grandeur
I just want to be me
To know what really matters and to live for that![1]

Introduction

Each generation must consider what it means to be distinctive as a Christian in their given context. The same applies in our celebrity-orientated world, where the question of success is particularly relevant. How we define success and how we live out our faith will inevitably impact how people perceive the claims that we make.

At times, I have felt alone in asking these questions. I chose to write because I wanted to explore the issues further. As someone in her twenties, I also thought that this would be an encouragement to my peers. I have discovered through writing that I am not alone in asking these questions. I do not claim to have all the answers but I am seeking to understand, and this process has helped!

I know that some will perceive my writing as an attempt to live out my own 'illusions of grandeur'. People will believe what they choose to, but this has never been my intention – as you will soon discover. My hope is that in exploring this together, we might all be challenged to increasingly put our faith into action.

Because life is full of complexities and challenges, this book is written around a narrative. The central figure is the biblical character of Joseph. Joseph's life was far from mundane or usual, but he demonstrates what it means to live through earthly success and through real challenges. His life is so extreme that it discourages us from being prescriptive, while encouraging us to seek to learn from the story.

I have no intention of writing a biblical commentary on the story of Joseph as there are plenty of excellent ones available. I have tried to focus on the question of success while drawing on the biblical story as the source of inspiration and challenge. Using stories of people living around the world today, including my own, I have tried to help relate the issues to our current context.

Each chapter is based on a different part of the Joseph story (Genesis 37–50). This is indicated in the chapter heading so that the reader can reflect on the biblical passage and so see whether they agree with my interpretation. These chapters begin with a quote from the text and a summary of the story so far. This is then followed by the experience of a contemporary and a reflection on the implications for the way we live.

This book is designed to be read by individuals but can also be explored in a group context. For this reason, I have added small-group material at the back of the book. As each group is different, the material outlines a number of options. Some are more creative, others are more discussion-based in style – you choose the style that works best for your group.

The aim of this format is to keep the biblical text at the centre whilst considering issues relevant to today's context. If Scripture is indeed God's word for God's world then my hope is that this will lead us all from thought into action. May we always be a people who authentically live out what we claim to believe.

Vicky Calver
Wimbledon, London
August 2005

1 Yearning for more

(*Genesis* 49:22–26)

A prince among his brothers (*Genesis* 49:26).

JOSEPH IS THE YOUNGER brother who thought he could surpass the rest. He is the dreamer with big dreams. He aspires to be a prince – anything other than the frog! His story is loved by those who feel the same way. Particularly as all this will one day be achieved – but not in the way he anticipated.

I know Helen well. She was scarcely your average teenager because Helen had dreams; not about wealth and position but about significance. As a pastor's kid, she had heard numerous sermons on the subject of living a life that makes a difference. She knew the stories. She had also listened to other people's comments and was excited by the possibilities of what her life could be. Her concern for the poor even made her wonder if she would be the next Mother Theresa!

Through the years, Helen grew both in faith and academic ability. By university, she had settled into the rhythm of debating the foundations of Christianity, while being absolutely sure that she now understood them. In the midst of this certainty, her parents became convinced that God was calling them to a new sphere of Christian service – but in the USA. As she took her finals, her parents packed up their home and prepared to leave.

No longer was Helen the only one following God into the unknown. Her parents went in one direction and she in another. For the next five years, she would live in four continents. She would work on behalf of the poor in India, Kenya and Rwanda, and would study for a Masters in the USA. Eventually she felt God's prompting to return home to the UK.

While overseas her certainty about life had been shaken. She had sat with people dying of AIDS, and had held a child who was literally starving to death. She had faced some of the complexities of life yet ultimately still expected all the pieces of *her* life to fit neatly together. After all, that was how all the great stories ended!

Returning to the UK proved to be a shock. She had followed God around the world; now she expected that he would give her a smooth transition back. But it was not to be. The months of readjustment plodded on as she sought to become established in the land that was still supposed to be her home. In time, she got temporary work and a room in a shared flat, but she was bored and restless. After ten months, she was offered a one-year contract working with HIV positive Africans in London. The work was stretching and interesting, but even this ended. She completed the year but the project could not be extended due to limited funds.

So now she found herself unemployed again. At the same time, one of her flatmates moved out and they struggled to find a replacement. The three remaining women had to cover the cost of the extra room or find themselves homeless. It was a tough time for Helen. Everything she had expected did not happen. No one seemed to want her! She found herself signing on with temping agencies, filling out application forms and waiting for phone calls.

Within a few days, she was offered two days' work distributing leaflets for a department store's Christmas sale. It was hardly stretching, nor what Helen felt she was capable of, but it was the only option available. Determined to work hard regardless of the mundane nature of the work, she trudged the London streets putting leaflets through letter boxes. Finally she was asked to stand on a street corner by the train station and distribute leaflets to passing commuters.

Many people walked past without a glance in Helen's direction. She felt shunned and irrelevant. Some took a leaflet but none smiled. Finally one gentleman stopped amidst the crowds and started talking to Helen. She was surprised but appreciated the diversion. He asked her whether this was the kind of work she would like to do long term. She said nothing but thought of the responsibilities that she had had only a week before. He then spoke of his work and suggested there might be some opportunities there. Helen was sceptical about his intentions but answered politely. As the gentleman moved away, he half turned and said, "You are literate, aren't you?"

If this were you, how would you respond? I was furious. Now Helen is no fictional character. Her story is my story, her dreams are my dreams and her questions are my questions. Helen is my middle name. I am Helen.

We all have dreams. For some it is being a professional footballer, for others it is being married with children, or climbing Mount Everest, or being a millionaire, a teacher or a film star. It may relate to job, position, achievements, wealth, or status. There is an assumption that success is achieving this goal. It is about big ambitions in acceptable categories. It is about fulfilling our dreams.

Now Joseph had big dreams. He dreamed of power and authority. His brothers would bow down to him. He would be acknowledged and respected. He would be a 'prince among his brothers' (Genesis 49:26). How tempting for us to dream in a similar way, and many of us do. Yet Joseph was to learn that life does not always work out as he expected.

I had to learn a similar lesson when I was asked if I was literate. This moment both crushed my self-esteem and taught me an essential lesson. I had so wanted to be valued and accepted and to have a 'significant' role. In many ways, I had a superhero view of life. I would swoop in and help others. I had built up the image that I could save the day, but was quickly discovering that others didn't view it that way. As my illusions of grandeur shattered, I started to ask what is really important in life.

Yet like me, how many of us have developed elaborate illusions of grandeur that are more about our own ego than anything else? We may be completely oblivious to the underlying assumptions of our actions, yet they reflect what we are really living for.

Dreams contain the hope of what could be and provide us with something to aim at, while illusions function more as a distortion and distraction. If I dreamed of swimming in my own pool then this could be an incentive to work to build one. Yet if I saw a mirage and thought it was a pool of water, I would get a shock if I tried to swim in it! In this way our dreams and illusions may be closely linked, yet function differently. One may cause us to want to achieve something; the other may lead us to believe that we already have.

This is brilliantly depicted in the film *Phone Booth*. It is the story of Stu Shepard, a 'successful' publicist. He wears smart clothes, looks good, has a wife and a girlfriend, and is followed around by a trainee. In keeping his affair secret from his wife, he calls his girlfriend from a phone booth rather than on a mobile. It is as he leaves the phone booth that the phone starts ringing and he makes the choice to pick it up. From that moment, the illusion of his happy and successful life shatters as the man on the other end of the phone says that he has a gun pointed at Stu and will kill him. As Stu re-evaluates his life, he starts to look at what really counts. Finally he admits to his wife:

> I think I need these clothes and this watch. My two-thousand-dollar watch is a fake and so am I. I neglected the things I should have valued most ... I've been dressing up as something I'm not for so long. I'm so afraid you won't like what's underneath. But here I am, just flesh and blood and weakness.[2]

How many of us, if we are really honest, would echo what Stu says? Stu had trusted his external image to hide his fears and concerns. He had not allowed himself to be vulnerable. He had lost the dream and was left with the illusion. Yet in sharing it with his wife he had the potential both to forgive himself and be forgiven, and so be restored.

Dreams are not static and may change with time. Yet as we get older, it is easy to become cynical and look down on our dreams. Some people seem to fulfil their dreams with few difficulties while others appear to have a much more circuitous route. The challenge is that many of our dreams include deadlines. We expect to have achieved certain things by a particular age and when this doesn't happen, we are left in crisis. This pressure has led Damian Barr to suggest that

> Feeling you should be having, doing or being more is the core of the 'quarterlife crisis'. Suddenly, 30 is so close you can smell it and everyone is doing better than you (or seems to be). The excitement of graduation fades. Real life sets in. And it's expensive, ugly

and competitive … We feel, even though we're only twenty-something, that our lives are in crisis. Why? Property has never been more expensive, work has never been so insecure and debt has never been so pervasive … If as we are told, the world is our oyster, it's definitely a dodgy one.[3]

If our experiences resonate with this, then we may face the challenge of disillusionment as our expectations fail to match our reality. If our circumstances do not match this then we may wonder what all the fuss is about. Either way, there is the question of whether our dreams reflect the life that we should be heading for. There is a danger that we will get to the end of our lives and discover that we wasted our efforts on what we thought was important but which didn't really count.

In our achievement-orientated world, success appears to be measured by numbers: the value of our possessions; our weight on the scales; the amount in our wallet; our grades in exams; whether we have a partner and children; or the number of promotions we have received. We divide the world into haves and have-nots, or even people who have some or have more. If we are haves or have-mores then we are successful; if we don't we aren't.

This is not to suggest that we should live without dreams. To do so would be to reduce life to a series of mechanical actions in order to survive. What a potentially miserable existence and what a waste! Our dreams can enable us to look beyond our current situation. They give us something to aim for and can provide us with a glimmer of hope.

The challenge is not whether we should dream, but what we should dream about. Subconsciously we can build our lives on that which we perceive to be important to those around us, rather than question what really matters and who we would like to become. As Christians, we may have accepted the value system of our culture rather than measure ourselves against the standards of a holy God.

We may dream, but are our dreams big enough to reflect the values of the God we claim to love? We only have one life. Each of us needs to be careful how we invest ours.

2 Glory seekers

(*Genesis* 37:1–11)

Now Jacob loved Joseph more that any of his other
children because Joseph had been born to him in
his old age. So one day he gave Joseph a special
gift – a beautiful robe. But his brothers hated
Joseph because of their father's partiality. They
couldn't say a kind word to him (Genesis 37:3,4).

THE CURTAIN RISES on the first scene of Joseph's story. It is
the story not of an individual but a family. The key character is
a teenager, whose very attitude and approach to life suggest
that he's a spoiled brat – either that or he's very naïve! Despite being one of 11 brothers, Joseph is his father's favourite.
He knows he is loved, he has the coat to prove it and now he
starts having dreams just to confirm it!

———— ◦ ◦ ————

Will knew what it was to feel rejected. His dad loved his mum,
but his older stepbrother ruined everything. Robin was really
angry with his dad for finding someone else and basically
forced his dad to choose between him and his new love. Will
and his mum lost and his dad returned to live with Robin.

Years later, Will is in a gang and his path crosses with his past. Robin turns up and joins the gang but he doesn't recognise Will. Yet again his brother barges in and takes over. Again, Will feels like his life is being dictated by his brother. But over time he begins to trust and even like Robin.

However, the truce is fragile. Eventually the relationship takes a turn for the worse and there is an argument. In frustration and confusion, Robin asks, 'Where does this intolerable hatred for me come from?' Will answers, 'Knowing that our father loved you more than me.'[4]

While the story of Will may be fiction (it comes from the film *Robin Hood, Prince of Thieves*), the sentiment for many is real. If we are really honest, are there not times when we have looked at others and asked the same question: whether they are more loved by parents, friends or God than we are? Their life seems so easy but ours is so complicated. Somehow beneath the concept that the evidence of success is seen in possessions or achievements, there can be a deep-seated and yet often unspoken assumption, that really these people are just more loved. They are the favourites and that's why life works out for them.

This was a key issue in the story of Joseph. His father loved him more and it was obvious to everyone else! Jacob's own family was torn apart by favouritism. Jacob's brother Esau was loved by his father, Isaac, while Jacob was the favourite of his mother, Rebekah. Jacob now repeats the actions of his parents by having a favourite son.

This family environment provides an interesting context for Joseph's dreams. History reveals that these dreams were prophetic, but at the time his brothers may have wondered whether God was also ganging up on them! This is where seeing God through the image of our own family causes us to misunderstand who God is. At this moment, Joseph's brothers may well have been wondering if God had favourites: their dad did! Yet God cannot be squeezed into the limits of our understanding. He does not always seem to act as we expect or like, but we do not understand everything. When it comes to whether or not God has favourites, the Bible affirms that God does not (Romans 2:11; Acts 10:34) and neither should his followers (James 2:1)!

However, Jacob does not follow God's example, and Joseph is caught in the crossfire. It is unclear the degree to which Joseph was consciously aware of the tensions with his brothers. In some senses he fuelled the situation by telling tales on them (v 2) but this could have been a reflection of normal sibling rivalry. To blame Joseph for the love that he received from his father seems harsh. According to the story, it is their father who gives Joseph a cloak to symbolise his special affection. Yet the brothers react with hatred towards their brother rather than their father. Perhaps Joseph was an easy target for their hatred, or maybe they thought that if Joseph wasn't there their father would love them all equally?

Human relationships are complicated. We all need to feel loved and accepted and in many ways, possessions or gifts can become symbolic. Like Joseph's cloak, it is possible to view material items as evidence that we are more important, loved or valued than others. Does this explain some of our assumptions about what success looks like?

Success is partly culturally defined, but our view of it may be influenced by our families. At the time of Joseph's story, the eldest child had a significant and important role because they inherited the family property. Yet Jacob broke this rule. If Jacob had given the coat to Reuben there may have been less tension because this would have been what was expected. By this single action, Jacob identifies Joseph as the heir – no wonder his brothers are consumed with jealousy! Similarly, we may value some things because they fit with what is seen as important in our family or among our peers. They may not be so important (or even be considered at all significant in the broader culture in which we live). But to us they are priceless.

Then again there is also the contrast between our expectations of ourselves, and the expectations of us that others hold. It may be that what drives us is our own will and determination. We have a sense of who we think we should be so we push ourselves towards that goal. It may be that we feel the sense of expectation much more from other people, whether family, friends or broader society. We use our energy to seek to be all that we think they want us to be. However, life is complex. Expectations can come from a variety of sources and we may not always be able to distinguish the conflicting motives so as to identify the source of the pressure.

Illusions of grandeur may then reflect our false expectations of what is significant. For example, someone with clear creative skills may not value their gift or feel looked down on, in a family, culture and/or among friends that value academic qualifications. Yet to be creative is a gift and something to be valued. Where our skills do fit our surrounding family's, peers' or culture's expectations of what is important or good, the illusion may be to overestimate our significance in the light of these gifts. Can it then be suggested that real success is having an appropriate view of ourselves and our gifts?

For Joseph, it now gets worse. He brags about himself. He sees his special position in the family as not only reflected in the favouritism of his father or the special cloak, but also in his dreams. From the brothers' point of view this is the ultimate illusion of grandeur. Joseph, the second to last child, dreams that all his brothers' bundles of grain bow down to his bundle. Then he dreams that the sun, moon and eleven stars bow down to him. In telling his brothers about the dream, Joseph could be seen by his brothers to be expounding his illusions of grandeur. You can just hear the potential arrogance of the statement and the way his brothers' blood would boil at the implication that they would be so beneath their little brother. The brothers respond in mockery, 'So you are going to be our king, are you?' (v 8). This simply covers up their jealousy and hatred. Jealousy can develop easily enough without the added fuel of grandiose dreams!

Yet is this what was going on? Were the dreams a projection of Joseph's ego, or is his reaction more to do with a naïve excitement? It is possible that Joseph had no big plans in his mind but that these dreams came from God. In his enthusiasm he shared this with his family with no awareness of the consequences. He was simply young and amazed at what God had revealed to him. His naïveté might seem cute to us, but was nearly fatal for him in the context of his brothers' emotions.

The passage does not tell us the source of the dreams nor why they were given. If they were a heavenly gift, then this may have been to give Joseph hope during the years of confusion ahead. The dreams could act as a promise of an unexpected ending, but they could equally have felt like a mockery. If there was truth in the dreams then Joseph could have felt like a failure in comparison, and humiliated by the presumption of them. The dreams suggested a life that would be so far from reality for Joseph for so many years that he may have wished he had never had them, for they only emphasised the negatives of his situation.

These dreams may have had a positive or a negative effect on Joseph, but it is possible that they were never really intended for him to think about. It could be that God revealed them to Joseph for Jacob's benefit not his. As the father, Jacob would be deeply impacted by all that would happen in the days ahead. The promise of the dream may have been more to give Jacob hope amidst his grief. Although Jacob challenges Joseph's assumption that they would all bow down to him, Scripture does tell us that he 'gave it some thought and wondered what it all meant' (v 11). Yet it is questionable how much he relied on the dreams once he was led to believe that Joseph had died. Naturally Jacob was heart-broken, but if the dreams were really intended for him he did not seem to learn the lessons from them.

Shark Tale is a cartoon about Oscar, a lowly fish with big dreams. During the day he works as a 'tongue-scrubber' at the 'Whale Wash', but as he cleans the tongues of his various customers, he dreams up the next get-rich-quick scheme. He eventually gets himself into financial difficulties and ends up talking with Angie, the receptionist who fancies him. He begins to explain why he is always daydreaming and seeking to earn more money. His father had been a tongue-scrubber before him and Oscar had been very proud of him. One day at show-and-tell at school he told the class of his dad and how much he wanted to be like him, but the other kids laughed at him. From that moment, Oscar no longer wanted to follow his dad; instead he wanted to be at the 'top of the reef'. The reason was that Oscar wanted to be a 'somebody, not a nobody'.[5]

How easy it is to be sucked into the lie that we only have value when we live in the right place, earn the best salary, spend time with the beautiful people etc! Yet there is a question here about our motivation. Oscar wanted to get to the top of the reef in order to be valued. Our hopes for the future may say a lot about our motivation and not just our direction.

In Christian circles, there seem to be few people who really talk about ambition. It is as if this is something that people shouldn't think about or shouldn't have, and yet the dreams that Joseph had certainly sound ambitious!

The Bible often appears to hold different issues in tension. The apostle Paul says, 'My ambition has always been to preach the Good News where the name of Christ has never been heard, rather than where a church has already been started by someone else' (Romans 15:20); and yet in the letter to the Galatians lists 'selfish ambition' (Galatians 5:20) as a negative quality. Similarly in the letter to the Philippians we read, 'Don't be selfish; don't live to make a good impression on others. Be humble; thinking of others as better than yourself.' (Philippians 2:3). Then he adds, 'Don't think only about your own affairs, but be interested in others, too, and what they are doing' (Philippians 2:4). James states, 'But if you are bitterly jealous and there is selfish ambition in your hearts, don't brag about being wise.' Then he explains why: 'That is the worst kind of lie. For jealousy and selfishness are not God's kind of wisdom' (James 3:14).

There is a real distinction between 'ambition' that is linked to selfishness, and ambition that benefits others. So often our concepts of success are about individual power, prestige, financial gain and achievements. If we are ambitious for personal gain then these passages suggest that we are chasing after that which is 'not God's kind of wisdom'. The question is not only *what* we are ambitious for, but *why*.

Our failure to distinguish between these types of ambition can limit our ability to have big dreams. A family friend of mine often talks about being 'greedy for God' and not just ourselves. We need to examine ourselves and our motivations so that we are sure our desires are rooted in a vision for God's glory and not our own. Yet if we run from anything that appears to be ambitious, we may equally be displaying self-centredness because we are focused on how we appear, rather than on what God could do. For some it is natural to have a big vision, for others it is not. But like the Psalmist, we all need to ask God both to search us and to lead us (Psalm 139:23,24) so that what we do is for the glory of his name and not just to enhance our own reputations!

The beginning of Joseph's story can be quite uncomfortable reading. In one sense it describes all the tensions and challenges that can exist in relationships whether we want to talk about them or not. On the other hand, it raises a lot of questions about how God relates to the issue of success. If the dreams came from God, then this would suggest that God had designs for Joseph's life that probably went way beyond Joseph's designs for his own life. Once the dreams are fulfilled, it is Joseph who affirms this by recognising that what his brothers meant for evil, God meant for good (Genesis 50:20).

The life of Joseph affirms that there is a sense of purpose even when everything is confusing and apparently meaningless. The issue for Joseph was whether his ultimate position and prestige would be for his personal benefit or for others. At the end, he affirms that God has allowed this so that his family would survive. Who do we want to benefit from our hopes and dreams? That is the challenge. We may use words about benefiting others in public but – in the secret of our own heart – who do we really want to gain from any prestige, power or wealth that we receive in life?

The challenge for Joseph was to trust God with the future. This is not to suggest that Joseph was fatalistic; he would need an active trust to enable him to serve Potiphar and the jailer yet hold on to a promise that would seem completely unrealistic. It could have been that these dreams would become the thing that Joseph would invest his life in trying to live up to, but his circumstances as a slave and a prisoner would not allow this.

Also, it would seem that Joseph learned what it was to trust God with the outcome. At various stages in Joseph's story, we read that God was with him. If Joseph had not trusted God, he may never have got through the confusion and silence of the coming years.

There is a similar challenge for us. We may not have had grandiose dreams or prophetic words said about our futures but that is not the issue. The challenge as followers of Jesus is whether we are prepared to trust God with our future. We may have dreams and ambitions for our life but these may simply be a reflection of what we consider worthy of praise. The real issue is who we trust to lead us.

I love books. In every book that my dad has given me, he has written the same biblical reference – John 2:5. It is what Mary says to the servants at the wedding of Cana when the wine runs out and Mary persuades Jesus to help. She says to the servants, 'Do whatever he tells you.' This has been the one thing that my dad has consistently challenged me to do in my faith. It is not comfortable and certainly doesn't make for a simple life, but it is part of the adventure of faith. To trust that God knows what he is doing and for us to walk in obedience, seeking to hear where he is leading, is the greatest challenge and can lead us to places we would never have dreamed of! They may not be grand in other people's eyes but if we know we are where God wants us to be, is that not enough?

3 Vying for attention

(*Genesis* 37:12–35)

'Here comes that dreamer!' they [Joseph's brothers]
exclaimed. 'Come on, let's kill him and throw him
into a deep pit. We can tell our father that a wild
animal has eaten him. Then we'll see what becomes
of all his dreams' (*Genesis* 37:19,20)!

THE DESTRUCTION in Joseph's family seems complete. Hatred has eaten into the relationship to such an extent that Joseph's brothers are ready to kill him. Meanwhile Joseph sets off to fulfil his father's wishes in apparent ignorance that anything will befall him. The division between this young, beloved son and his angry, resentful brothers is clear. The time for the showdown has come.

It had been a busy day. I was visiting some friends for the evening, so we sat talking as the sun set. Eventually our conversation turned to Joseph. I shared how I thought that being innocently sent to jail was the most difficult thing Joseph experienced. My friend turned and said, 'Forget the prison; it's the well that counts!'[6]

Initially I was taken aback. Why the well? Then it dawned on me, I was in Rwanda. My friend, Ngoga, was Rwandan and

35

although he had not lived through the genocide firsthand he had plenty of friends who had. He knew much more about the reality and impact of betrayal than I could even comprehend.

It took his words to make me realise how difficult this situation was for Joseph. His brothers discarded him as if he had nothing to do with them. They ignored their family history, betrayed him, threatened him with death, left him in a cold, lonely place wondering what would happen next and then sold him to foreigners who would take him to live permanently in another land.

This moment is not just about Joseph. His brothers had watched their father lavish his affection on their brother, not them. The special cloak was merely a symbol of what they had presumably had to witness and endure for months, if not years. It's not even as if Joseph was the eldest, which would have at least made the situation more socially acceptable. No, he was the second youngest and these men are overwhelmed by their jealousy and anger.

Love was the prize and success was gaining their father's affection. We don't know what methods the brothers employed to gain their father's love. Were they scheming to gain their father's attention when Joseph told tales about them? However, it quickly becomes apparent that they are vying for his attention. Eventually they conclude that the only way they will ever have a chance of gaining their father's love is by removing their competitor.

The tragedy is that the desire to be loved can at once be such a prize and such a cause of destruction. This is not only a challenge in Joseph's family but can face many. Siblings often compete for their parents' attention. Single people can feel that they are somehow not so significant because someone has not openly declared their love for them in a wedding ceremony. People in loveless relationships can feel marginalised and undermined. It would seem that love itself can be used as a weapon to affirm our worth in the eyes of others. We may suggest that to be loved is to be successful.

But what about those who feel unloved? Joseph's brothers are an illustration of what can happen. They are consumed by their jealousy. This emotion eats at them until they cannot understand the situation from any other angle. Their father was wrong in his affection for one over the others, but they made a choice in letting the situation go to the extreme that it did.

The challenge was that they were striving for something that they could not gain through competition. Unlike Joseph, God does not have favourites. His love is big enough to embrace us all. He has taken the initiative and wants to draw us near to him. As humans, we have sought to go our own way and have chosen not to live within the intentions of the God who loves us. We get caught up in striving for other things rather than resting in God's love and learning to follow him in obedience.

One of the most amazing truths in our world (if not *the* most amazing truth) is that through the death and resurrection of Jesus, we are now able to come back to God. We do not come in pride, but in sorrow for our rejection of him. We do not bring our good deeds, but the reality of our failures. God longs to embrace us, but we often prefer to strive stubbornly for his affection rather than rest in it. As we come in surrender of ourselves to a King who comes to reign in our lives, we find new life – not just for now but for eternity!

Knowing that we are loved can enable us to feel secure and so provides a positive environment in which we can flourish. It is not necessary to strive for something that is there. We have a choice. Will we spend our whole life fighting to gain what is offered freely? Whatever our home situation is like, whatever our family background, whatever our weaknesses, fears, errors, wrong-doing – God stands with arms open wide. The question is, will we run into them or past them?

I have often imagined a large hand. In the middle of the hand is a tiny child. But she has crawled to the edge of the hand and is looking down the gap between the thumb and the palm. A wave of panic hits her as she imagines falling down the hole. She feels lost and alone. She is safe in the middle of the hand and if she only looked up she would see a loving face. But she doesn't.

Sound familiar? There are so many things that can distract us. There can be so much noise in the way we live that we may battle to hear God. We can get so busy with activity – even when that activity is called pleasure! We may feel under pressure from people, debt, or our own expectations. All these things can cloud how we see things.

We chase after our illusions of grandeur – those things that we think we need in order to have value and significance. But in our hurry to fulfil our dreams for our own lives, we can lose sight of what really counts. If we learned to listen to and follow after the God who loves us and wants us to know him, then our approach to life would be different even if much of what we did was the same. God calls us to this new life amidst all our activity – 'Be still, and know that I am God' (Psalm 46:10, NIV).

For Joseph's brothers, in their pain, their only prospect was to remove its source. To betray their brother in this way may sound like poetic licence on the part of the author. Surely things wouldn't have happened like this! But our idealism is checked by films like *Schindler's List* and *Hotel Rwanda*, which remind us of periods of history when betrayal was a death sentence for many. This is not simply something that happened in the past but that continues today in particular parts of the world.

The danger with only seeing betrayal on the large scale is that it enables us to ignore the potential that we might betray others. In nations where success is understood as the achievements of an individual, are we not equally tempted to betray each other in our attempt to compete against each other for recognition, financial gain and even love? This can be done on multiple levels.

In *California Dreaming*, a recent reality TV show, a would-be film writer went to see an 'expert' about how to develop his career. The 'expert' kept saying, 'Don't tell me your idea. I'm sure it is a good one but if you tell me I might use it.'[7] This may illustrate the temptation that we all face. Betrayal is masked by the benefit to the individual even if the impact is felt by other individuals. In our hurry to gain more, whether status, money or relationships, there is the danger that we may hurt others. Betrayal need not just be out there – it can be a trap that we fall into unconsciously or consciously.

Joseph's brothers did this in various ways. Some were happy to take matters into their own hands and get rid of Joseph by 'any means necessary'. Reuben, the eldest, appealed to their logic in order to plan a way to rescue Joseph (vs 21,22). Yet when his plan failed, he did not have the courage to either chase after the traders to buy his brother back, or go to his father and honestly tell him what happened. Reuben had tried to live differently to his siblings but he was guilty because of his passive involvement. He could have stopped it – he didn't. He did prevent the death of his brother, but disappeared while Joseph still needed him. His silence allowed their father to think Joseph was dead. Lifelong slavery could have been the result if God had not stepped in.

The other brother mentioned specifically is Judah. He appealed to his brothers' sense of guilt to remove Joseph without killing him. Then the brothers set out to deceive their father by soaking Joseph's cloak in the blood of a goat. They let their father think the worse. The brothers end up acting together even if not every member was directly involved. Their silence before their father meant that they were all implicated.

It is at this moment that history appears to repeat itself. Jacob, their father, had obeyed his mother and deceived his father. He had pretended to be his older brother in order to gain the blessing reserved for the eldest son (Genesis 27:1–41). Now he experiences a similar deception. He doesn't question his assumptions or his sons; rather he is overwhelmed by grief. If Joseph's brothers thought that this was the ultimate way to get their father's attention, they were wrong. In his apparent death, Joseph has even more influence!

There may be situations where we are tempted to turn a blind eye. It may put our job at risk to say something or cause our colleagues to react against us. Therefore to maintain our position and power, it seems better to do nothing; but this in itself can be to do something! This scenario questions how much we are prepared to do to gain or keep our position.

Yet even betrayal does not put us beyond God's love. Peter was one of the twelve, a close friend of Jesus. He was the first to acknowledge Jesus as Messiah (Mark 8:29); he was one of three witnesses chosen to witness Jesus transformed and walking around with Elijah and Moses (Mark 9:2–8); and he was picked by Jesus to watch and pray during the final hours in the Garden of Gethsemane (Mark 14:32–34). Despite all this, Peter betrayed Jesus. He had declared fervently that he wouldn't (Mark 14:29–31), but when the time came he would deny Jesus three times (Mark 14:66–72). Yet as the cock crowed a second time, Peter would realise what he had done and be completely distraught. But this was not the end of the story.

At the resurrection, the angels would specifically mention

Peter as one of the disciples who should receive Jesus' message (Mark 16:7). And on the shore of the Sea of Galilee, Jesus would come to Peter and affirm the responsibility that he has been given over the church (John 21:15–19). As Jesus had said earlier, 'Now I say to you that you are Peter, and upon this rock I will build my church' (Matthew 16:18). Peter betrayed Jesus yet he received forgiveness. If we come in repentance and faith, we will also receive this forgiveness. Betrayal does not put us beyond God's love.

Like Peter, Joseph's life affirms that forgiveness to actions that seem unforgivable is possible. Yet it has a price. Unlike Peter, Joseph is not the one needing forgiveness but the one who is to give it. If we could fully comprehend the agony of this moment for Joseph, it would give us much greater insight into the amazing moment of forgiveness nearer the end of the story.

4 Valuing the ordinary

(*Genesis* 37:36; 39:1–5)

The LORD was with Joseph... (*Genesis* 39:2).

JOSEPH IS BANISHED from his home by his own brothers. He goes from being a carefree, secure and even arrogant teenager to a young man abandoned by his family, led away by foreigners and sold as a slave into the home of a wealthy man in a strange land. And all by the time he was 17!

Joseph's dreams are shattered, and presumably they stay in his memory as a painful reminder of what could have been. The most loved son must now face the isolation and loneliness of abandonment. We can only imagine the pain, confusion and possible despair of these early days in Potiphar's household.

———————

Despair is a strange experience. It is like sitting and staring into a black hole: a downward spiral of inward pain and confusion that seems to have no end. In 2002, I returned to the UK – my fourth continent in five years. I thought I was coming 'home' but quickly discovered that I had no home. I had left the country in 1997, after finishing my degree, to work among street children in India. At the same time my parents had moved to the USA. In the intervening years, I had got an MA in the USA and had spent two years working with people living with HIV/AIDS in Kenya and Rwanda. Now I was back in the UK and trying to make sense of my life.

On my return, I had expected enthusiasm among my friends, but it seemed that they quickly forgot I was around. I had assumed that, unlike the other places I lived, everything would suddenly make sense in England; but I was wrong. Subconsciously I had thought I would fall into a great job and have the responsibility I needed, yet all the comments from recruitment agencies suggested that I was unusual and work would not be easy to find.

My aunt and uncle were amazing. I lived with them while I worked out what I should do next. But I missed my family home and the life I remembered. My parents phoned regularly but I could not live with them as they were in the USA. My brothers were happily settled. I was the oldest but felt like the youngest. Everything I thought was secure and made sense suddenly didn't.

Eventually I got a job and found a flat with other single, professional women, but something from those four months of confusion lingered. The job was not the most inspiring as I became a close friend of the filing cabinet! I worked hard because I believed that would honour God, but inwardly I felt like I was dying. I felt sure that I was made for more than this. I felt crushed and disillusioned, emotional and hurting.

Then one Sunday I met with my brother, Gavin, for lunch. Through my tears, I shared my confusion about how I could work for God overseas and yet he had abandoned me when I needed him most. I was trying to cling to my crumbling faith while struggling not to become bitter. I felt the unfairness of my situation. I had expected certain things from life and from God and none of it was happening. Eventually, Gavin spoke up. Rather than sympathy or encouragement, he chose to challenge me with words I'll never forget. He said, 'How you respond now will affect who you become.'[8]

It was like a bolt of lightening. Suddenly I realised life didn't have to be like this. I had been caught up in my expectations of what life should be like. Gavin's comment pulled me up short and made me realise that I had a choice in how to respond. I needed to value each day and enjoy just living. I could choose to stop dreaming of how my life should be, fuelling my own illusions, and seek to trust God even when nothing made sense rationally.

Because of this, in the months that followed, God began to reveal his faithfulness to me. At times I clung to the biblical promises about God's presence through sheer determination. But as I sought to live each day, giving it to God and not worrying about tomorrow, I discovered more of God's peace. I realised that while I had felt lost and so far from God, he had been close. I could not see what was going on but God was at work in my heart and life, and others could see it. I started to discover that, as for Joseph, God was with me when things were tough.

There is no reference in the story of Joseph as to how he coped emotionally. There is no reason to assume that his experience was anything like mine, and yet his life was turned upside down when he was only 17. The narration at this moment in Joseph's story comes as a real encouragement to those of us who may struggle to see God in moments of real pain. For as one commentator says,

The name of Yahweh [usually translated as 'the LORD'] occurs here at what is the most uncertain moment in the life of Joseph. His future hangs in the balance. He is alone in Egypt, separated from family, vulnerable, with a cloud over his future. Or is he alone? Only the narrator who tells us, no less than five times, that in a very precarious situation, Joseph is not really alone.

Yahweh is with him.[9]

It is interesting that Joseph is never seen stating his knowledge of God's presence. It was obvious to Potiphar; was it so clear to Joseph? His feelings did not determine God's presence; God was there whether Joseph realised it or not. Joseph had a choice about how he would respond to his circumstances but not about whether God was there. This can be a challenge to us when life is overwhelming and we can no longer sense God's presence.

In the boredom of mundane jobs, in ill-health, in loneliness, in questions about the future, in disappointment or disillusionment it is easy to consider ourselves alone, and yet God is there. We may not always 'feel' it, but Scripture affirms that God is still there. In Psalm 139, David speaks of a variety of places that we could go to get away from God, but he ends up stating that it is not possible to escape from God's Spirit:

> I could ask the darkness to hide me
>> and the light around me to become night –
>> but even in darkness I cannot hide from you.
> To you the night shines as bright as day.
>> Darkness and light are both alike to you.
>> (*Psalm* 139:11,12)

The Bible says nothing of Joseph's emotions at this time, but it does state that he 'served in the home of his Egyptian master' (Genesis 39:2). He had the courage to get on with serving regardless of what he wanted or expected from life. He may have had little choice in the matter; after all, he was a servant! However, Joseph was given a lot of responsibility and so must have proved his character by the way he responded to the work that needed doing.

It seems that in these years of being a servant, Joseph kept putting one foot in front of the other; he kept serving and he kept working. He learned faithfulness in the day to day. This type of practical faith is a challenge for us, as Oswald Chambers suggests:

> We do not need the grace of God to withstand crises – human nature and pride are sufficient for us to face the stress and strain magnificently. But it does require the grace of God to live twenty-four hours of every day as a saint, going through drudgery, and living an ordinary, unnoticed, and ignored existence as a disciple of Jesus. It is ingrained in us that we have to do exceptional things for God – but we do not. We have to be exceptional in the ordinary things of life, and holy on the ordinary streets, among ordinary people – and this is not learned in five minutes.[10]

This is especially tough for us in our instant societies. Our expectations of what life should be like often don't include words like boring and frustrating. It is tempting to compare ourselves to others and consider the injustice of our situation. How can they be earning so much? Why am I not being used to my potential? And so on.

But, do we need to take our head out of the clouds and put our feet on the ground? How can I serve God and show my faith in this boring and unexciting situation? What does this mean for my work, relationships, leisure – every aspect of life?

Angela is a friend from university. When she was nine she was diagnosed with spinal curvature and at 13 she had surgery for a neurological condition. Ill-health has been part of her life ever since. Until her mid-twenties it was more an inconvenience than anything. Her mum used to say, 'Don't ask "why me?", ask "why not me?".'[11]

Those words used to irritate her as they didn't make any sense and certainly didn't answer her questions. Nowadays, in her late twenties, she values them because they stopped her from the self-pity that could have governed the two years that followed university when she was housebound.

Angela is as human as the rest of us, but her attitude to life is a real challenge. She is bubbly and chatty, when she has the energy to talk. She is positive about life, despite being an educated and capable young woman who faces the daily frustrations of not being able to do as much as she would like because of her health. She has not become trapped in her own needs but rejoices in the good things that are happening in other people's lives and is willing to help when she can, even if that means she has little energy the next day. She has learned to appreciate it when she can function and experiences God in the little things.

Like Joseph, Angela demonstrates the importance of living for others within the limitations of her circumstances. Yet many of us face the temptation of the rat race, of grabbing more and more for ourselves – a home, the latest gadgets, 'in' clothes, interesting experiences – yet what do we lose by our self-absorption? Jesus says, 'Whoever wants to be a leader among you must be your servant, and whoever wants to be first must become your slave. For even I, the Son of Man, came here not to be served but to serve others' (Matthew 20:26–28). If I want to follow Jesus, what implications does this have for the way I live my life?

It is tempting to think that if we seek to honour God by serving those around us then, like Joseph we will have 'success in everything' (Genesis 39:3). However, in Genesis 'there is no attempt to place Joseph on a pedestal or to single him out for acclaim. The source of Joseph's success is patently Yahweh's presence with him.'[12] This begs some questions. If God is with us then shouldn't we all be 'successful'?

There are people who hold to a belief in what is known as

the 'prosperity gospel' or 'name it and claim it' faith. They argue that God wants to give good gifts to his children, so if we have enough faith and trust God then he will bless us materially. The story of Joseph could be used to argue this position. God was with Joseph and blessed him and gave him success.

It is interesting that the success referred to is not Joseph's freedom or personal gain. The success is linked to his service and his ability to lead the household and his trustworthiness in business dealings. These would have led to the better running of the household and presumably some material benefits for Potiphar through his business. However, the Bible states that all of these blessings are linked to God and not Joseph's natural ability or hard work. God is developing gifts in Joseph that he will use in increasing ways for the good of the community in the days to come.

It is easy to think of faith as a quick fix. If we are obedient then God will automatically make everything OK. We seem to lack an understanding of what part suffering plays in our existence. We quote passages like 'God causes everything to work together for the good of those who love God' (Romans 8:28) as clichés, but seem to misunderstand the point. Ironically, many people in the Bible struggled and suffered, yet it was the making of them. Therefore, our attempts at pain avoidance may cause us to miss out on all that God would teach us. Watchman Nee, a Chinese Christian who faced imprisonment and suffering for his faith, highlights this for us:

> Revelation waits upon discipline … Every day God is looking for opportunities to enlarge us, but when difficulties arise we avoid them, when trials come we circumvent them. Oh but at what loss to ourselves! And at what loss to God's people![13]

As we learn to face the challenges of life with all its limitations and disappointments, we have the possibility of developing

49

in character and faith so that not only do we know God more but that others are helped through us. If we can learn to value the ordinary, the impact will be significant.

> We also rejoice in our sufferings, because we know that suffering produces perseverance; perseverance, character; and character, hope. And hope does not disappoint us, because God poured out his love into our hearts by the Holy Spirit, whom he has given us.
> (*Romans* 5:3-5, NIV)

5 Choosing to be different

(*Genesis* 39:6–20)

But Joseph refused… 'No one here has more authority than I do! He [Potiphar] has held nothing from me except you, because you are his wife. How could I ever do such a wicked thing? It would be a great sin against God' (*Genesis* 39:8,9).

JOSEPH HAS REACHED the pinnacle of his position. He remains a slave but has as much authority as he can be given at this stage. He has freedom and control of the household, but there are limits. Potiphar's wife is one of them; although she doesn't look at it this way. Joseph is young and good-looking, and she fancies him. She tries to persuade him to sleep with her but he's having none of it. A woman scorned is not a good prospect! Life is about to get much more interesting for Joseph…

In a London college, two teenagers meet and start dating. Mark considers himself to be a lucky guy. Lisa is one of those good-looking girls who everyone fancies, and she wants to be with him. Mark feels on top of the world. He is successful, he got the girl and all the other guys envy him. Life is good!

At the end of the two years, it's exam time. It takes a few

months for the results to come out and when they do life is suddenly not so good for Mark. Lisa gets a distinction in her GNVQ qualifications but Mark only gets a C, D and E in his A-levels. He knows he could have done better, but is baffled that she did so well. How could she be so successful in her exams, when they saw each other the same amount of time?

He was also baffled as to why he had done so badly. It began to dawn on him that maybe he had relied too much on the success he felt from being with Lisa, rather than on concentrating on doing well himself. She was obviously successful both in her exams and in the ways that others perceived her, but Mark had failed to gain such success in his own right. Mark came to see success not only in who he dated but in how well he did in his studies.

He decided to move to a different college that was further away and retake his exams so that he would be able to go to university. As he moved away from his former priorities, he became more focused. In one year, he was able to improve his grades from a D and E to a B and C in his retakes. As someone in his mid-twenties, Mark now suggests that we sometimes have to flee what we perceive to be success in order to really be successful.

Mark succeeded in getting Lisa to go out with him, but failed to achieve the grades he needed to continue in further education. Potiphar's wife succeeded in marrying a man who would give her a good position in life but failed to seduce Joseph. Joseph succeeded in resisting Potiphar's wife but failed to keep his privileged position. In each of these situations of apparent success there is an element of failure.

For Potiphar's wife, her failure and success were both based on relationships. It may have been that having gained status in marrying Potiphar, she needed a new challenge and Joseph was it. Her seduction of him may have been an opportunity for her to assert her own power and authority. As a slave, he would be subject to her and she orders him, 'Sleep with me' (v 12). The statement does not leave room for refusal or questions.

It would appear that the situation with Joseph was not just about power but also pleasure. Joseph is described as 'a very handsome and well-built young man' (v 6). Potiphar's wife is attracted to him. She starts by 'inviting him' to sleep with her. It is only later that she tries commanding him. If she had succeeded, she could also have used their pleasure as a weapon to make Joseph do what she wanted to prevent her from telling Potiphar. It sounds like a storyline from *Eastenders*!

This search for pleasure and power may well be the driving force behind much of our understanding of success. Why else are fast cars, expensive restaurants or powerful positions so praised? There may be other factors like beauty, but this can link with pleasure because an appreciation of beauty creates pleasure. If the suggestion that power and pleasure lie beneath many of our concepts of success then these things (cars, food, status etc) are the illusions that mask our deeper desires.

But are power and pleasure also diversions in thinking of success? For all her manipulative and demanding ways, Potiphar's wife could not gain the pleasure or power that she wanted simply by grasping for it. In many ways it is Joseph who is successful, as Potiphar's wife is left rejected and refused.

It may be that real success is linked to having a sense of purpose in our lives. Joseph knew that his role was to maintain the household and that to sleep with Potiphar's wife would be to abuse Potiphar's trust. He knew what he should do and was determined to live according to his own principles even if others thought he was crazy. Joseph demonstrates what it means to live for a different version of success, regardless of what those around us believe.

For Joseph, there was a clear sense of what was right and wrong before God and before Potiphar. He determined his actions not from his own preferences but by deciding what was right. He was either a teenager or a man in his early twenties at the time. Presumably he had set his principles before this incident; otherwise he probably would have gone with his sexual yearnings and slept with her. If this is the case, then there may be a challenge to us to think through our choices and decide our priorities.

Even when we know what we stand for, others may try to persuade us otherwise. Ultimately, Joseph had to flee from temptation. He had tried reasoning but if he stayed any longer he was in trouble. Like Joseph, we may find ourselves in situations when the only choice is to run away. The question is whether we go.

If you and I were asked what principles we had based our lives on, what would they be? Now, this is not just about principles in sexual behaviour, but rather the convictions that lie beneath our general behaviour shown in how we use our time, money, possessions and energy. It can be tempting to hide behind the convictions of others rather than determine how we will behave, but if we don't decide, then we will get pressured into doing what other people think is OK regardless of what we think.

However, some of the situations we find ourselves in are not clear-cut. Getting a promotion at work may be the ultimate success for us and yet it may mean we spend more time at work and have less time and energy to invest in our children, spouse, friends etc. It may be right for us to take the job but it may not be. It may be that we should take it but that we need to make some decisions about how to protect these other relationships. If we know what our priorities are and we are seeking to listen to God, then we are more likely to make choices that we think are appropriate regardless of whether they fit with the social norm.

Whatever choices we make, we will still live with the consequences of those actions and will need to work them through. Even in fleeing from Potiphar's wife in order to keep his integrity, Joseph still faced consequences: he lost his job and his freedom. Potiphar's wife had failed to get what she wanted, but now she twists the situation to turn the moment of her failure into a moment of triumph. She reverses the order of events. No longer is it she who grabs Joseph and then calls out to the servants once he has fled. Now she screams and then he flees. The action of grabbing and calling out are reversed with powerful effect. Her lie enables her to reassert her authority as there is no one to remind her of her failure. None of the servants saw the incident and Joseph is neatly removed.

When success is praised, it is often easier to change the perception of our failures by blaming others rather than learning from them. Potiphar's wife not only accused Joseph but subtly shifted the blame from herself to her husband for bringing Joseph in to the household (v 17). From childhood, there is a tendency to say, 'But it wasn't me, it was ...' As adults, do we admit it when we err? Do we try to turn the situation around so that we are not the culprit? Like Potiphar's wife, we will discover that how we handle our failures, will effect what we learn from them.

Recently a group of up-and-coming actors, actresses, singers and musicians went to Hollywood to try and make a name for themselves. They were part of a reality TV show, and so the group were staying in a luxury house and were being trained by an American talent spotter. At their first meeting, the talent spotter told the group that there are many actors, actresses, singers and musicians in Los Angeles and so it was important to know what unique abilities would make them stand out. Basically, did they have it in them to become a star?

The question for the group was what made them individually distinctive from everyone else who could do the same role. Distinctiveness is not just about outward appearance. Outwardly Joseph was distinctive as a foreigner, as Potiphar's wife reminds Potiphar in her accusation of Joseph. Yet what makes him really distinctive are his choices. He was not blinded by the appeal to power or pleasure in Potiphar's wife's proposal. He knew what principles governed his life and he was not prepared to disconnect his actions from his beliefs.

If we want to be successful in living up to the standards that we set ourselves, then we need to have the courage of our convictions. As Christians, the Bible can provide us with principles about how we should live, but we still have the choice of whether to follow them. Others may seek to dissuade us, but we have choices – we can try reason or fleeing. If success is living out what we claim to believe, then the distinctive for a Christian is the having the foundations of our convictions in the Bible. If we don't do this, we always run the risk of being hypocritical in our behaviour or being swayed by other people's attitudes and reactions.

The challenge, then, is whether we will have the courage of our convictions and so live out what we claim to believe. If we do this, we may discover that what outwardly appears to be failure may really be success!

6 Faithfulness rewarded

(*Genesis* 39:20–23)

He [Potiphar] took Joseph and threw him into the
prison where the king's prisoners were held. But
the LORD was with Joseph there, too, and he
granted Joseph favour with the chief jailer

(*Genesis* 39:20,21).

THINGS ARE GOING from bad to worse for Joseph. He may
have thought he was bottom of the food chain as a servant,
now he's a prisoner! In trying to do the right thing by not
sleeping with Potiphar's wife, he ends up even worse off.
There certainly doesn't seem to be any justice for Joseph.

———◦•◦———

Alison is 29 years old. She's been a Christian since she was
young. She suffered from glandular fever as a teenager but
once she recovered she got back into an active lifestyle. Then
at the age of 25 she felt God calling her to return to her home
church to be involved in youth work. She left her job, moved
back and started to set up a youth café. Things were developing well until the week before the café was due to open and
she contracted shingles.

Alison kept going but her health did not improve after

recovering from shingles. Eventually the doctors diagnosed her with fibromyalgia. Physically, she was no longer able to do what she had been doing. She would go to church on Sunday because she thought she should but then she would spend the next four days in bed recovering. It was not just the fatigue that got her down; the pain was like 'hot knitting needles through your bones'.

People started to ask why she had left her job and now couldn't even do the youth work. She even wondered that herself! Her identity had always been tied up with what she did. Now she couldn't do anything, she started to question who she was. She became depressed and started self-harming. Nothing made sense anymore. What made it even harder was that many people did not even believe that she was really sick because when they did see her she looked fine. They did not see the days when she couldn't get out of bed. They missed the daily struggles that had become part of her life.

Eventually the doctors admitted Alison to hospital for physio rehab. Because her illness was linked to arthritis, she found herself on a ward with 90-year-old women. As the hospital was so far from home, she would only get visits for an hour a day but the rest of the time she was alone. That first night as she wept, she felt God say, 'You've got to learn not to do anything, but I will always still be here.'

Those days in hospital were a real turning point. She couldn't cope with reading or listening to music, and even following the story line in Neighbours became a problem! What she could do was spend time in prayer and meditation. She began to discover what it means to spend time with God not in activity but in stillness. She started to learn that, 'I can be more than what I do.'[14]   She left hospital a changed woman.

Since then, Alison has had to increasingly learn to listen to God and her body before doing things. She lives with the constant restrictions of ill-health but they are lessening. Four years on, she is anticipating the opportunity of going back to work part-time. Alison still does not fully understand why she has been through all of this. Yet she recognises that if she hadn't been forced to stop, she never would have found the value of being and not just doing.

In many senses, Alison lives within a box created by her ill-health. In another way, she may have found a greater freedom than the rest of us! Success is no longer just about what she does. She has discovered a new meaning to her identity – one that is found in resting in God. In this way, the illusion that who Alison is, is defined by what she does, has been destroyed, giving her the freedom to explore alternative definitions for her identity. How many of us are bound by the same illusion?

For Joseph, prison was a literal cage. For Alison, ill-health has created an invisible one. Prisons are places where we live within certain restrictions that others may or may not see. There can be a deep sense of feeling trapped by circumstances, and the frustration and anger that comes from not being able to fix the situation easily. It may be a job that feels restricting and boring; a housing situation that is less than ideal without any realistic chance of changing it; a relationship that is a source of deep pain and confusion. Like Alison, others may not see the bars that hold us, and this can lead to a deeper sense of rejection and isolation.

Naturally, we want to flee the restrictions and escape the pain. But what can be learned in the darkness? I am not sure that even at the end of Joseph's story there is an easy answer as to why he had to endure years in prison. He did gain responsibilities in the jail and this may have been a good learning ground, but why prison and not somewhere else?

It may have been that this was a place where Joseph had

nothing else he could rely on. He was forced to choose how he would respond to the questions and confusion. He probably felt forgotten and yet people were still watching: his fellow prisoners, the chief jailer and God. Joseph was the only member of his tribe there. He was isolated and yet he could still reflect different values. His integrity could be buried in his anger after the incident with Potiphar's wife, or he could continue to seek to live a life of honour. Joseph had choices that would impact the rest of his life, even if the link was not always obvious to the naked eye.

There is something that happens through painful periods of time. Our questions can lead us to destructive behaviour and even suicide, but they can also lead us to deeper faith and greater certainty. It is like a cut on our skin. If it gets infected then it does not heal and can lead to further problems. But if the cut heals well, it leaves a scar. The composition of the skin in a scar takes on a more concrete form than the skin around it. It is less elastic than the rest of the skin but it is more solid and, in that sense, it is stronger after the cut than before. The scar remains as a reminder that there has been a cut, but there is strength in that reminder!

Likewise with us, painful periods may remain unresolved and may be like infected cuts that inhibit our ability to heal, and damage our future growth. Or painful periods can lead to scars that remind us of the pain but give us a strength that would not have been there before. This is not to idealise situations that are incredibly difficult. Skin needs elasticity and so the loss of elasticity in a scar is not necessarily good. But this is also not to undermine the truth that something can happen in pain that can provide a lasting strength that we can draw upon as we reach out to others with love and concern and as we seek to grow ourselves.

This is also reflected in Psalm 84:

Happy are those who are strong in the LORD,
   who set their minds on a pilgrimage to Jerusalem.
When they walk through the Valley of Weeping,
   it will become a place of refreshing springs,
   where pools of blessing collect after the rains!
They will continue to grow stronger
   and each of them will appear before God in Jerusalem.
      (Psalm 84:5,6)

We may not instantly see the 'pools of blessing'; we may not understand the 'Valley of Weeping'; but the issue is, have we set our minds on a pilgrimage to Jerusalem? I don't mean this in a literal sense. Jerusalem in Old Testament thinking was the place where God dwells. The question then is whether we have set our minds on following after God. Are we ready to be Christians who start to follow Jesus and not just each other? If we really took Jesus' words in the Gospels seriously, would we not have to change the way we live? Would we not have to rethink what is really important in life and what success looks like?

The great thing about the story of Joseph is that it is not all about him. We are reminded in these short verses that actually God was with Joseph. Whether he felt it or not, Joseph was not alone. A recognition of God's presence in difficult times has also been part of Alison's experience. Literal and invisible bars do not block God out. In pain and difficulties, we may choose to turn away from God, yet his presence is always there. He longs to draw people back to himself. The question is whether we will allow him to.

Whether prison was where Joseph wanted to be or not was irrelevant; it was where he was and God was there in the midst of it all. There are lots of things that happen to us, because of the actions of others or our own circumstances, that may cause us to feel helpless as we cannot control the outcome. Yet we can control our response to these situations.

This is clear in the story of *Lord of the Rings*. Frodo is a hobbit, one of the little people. He finds himself, by no fault of his own, in possession of the Ring of Power. He has a choice: he can seek to own the ring and be consumed by its power and ultimately give the power pack to the evil Sauron, or he can throw the Ring of Power into the fires of Mordor, thus destroying it and ending the control of Sauron over Middle Earth. The choice is not easy and it is one that Frodo never wanted to have to make. However, he is not alone. Three hobbits, two men, one dwarf, one elf and a wizard join him on the journey to destroy the ring. En route he talks with Gandalf, the wizard, about his struggles with having to deal with the ring:

'I wish it need not have happened in my time,' said Frodo.

'So do I,' said Gandalf, 'and so do all who live to see such times. But that is not for them to decide. All we have to decide is what to do with the time that is given us.'[15]

Within all the talk of finding strength in painful places, the bottom line for Joseph was that he got on with working where he was. Joseph's situation probably felt very unjust. All he had tried to do was serve Potiphar well and he found himself in prison. He could have spent his time dwelling on the injustice of the situation rather than getting on with life. He could have done the bare minimum required by a prisoner rather than doing his best. Actually, he must have chosen the latter option in order to have been recognised by the chief jailer.

Joseph learned to do a job well whatever the circumstances. He had influence and responsibility in unlikely places, and the smooth running of the prison was noted as a success. We do not always see the good administration of places like a prison, office, school, community hall as a mark of success, yet that is what the Bible says about the prison (v 23). Joseph's actions also meant that the chief jailer had nothing to worry about.

In many senses, the roles are reversed. Joseph has authority in the prison but remains a prisoner; he has the ability to do his boss's job yet remains in a lower position. As a prisoner, there was probably nothing Joseph could do about who got the credit for his work, but there is no reference to him slowing down or causing the chief jailer to have to start worrying again. As far as we know, Joseph simply continued working. He made the prison a success in that it ran well, but even this is attributed to God and not Joseph!

Joseph worked faithfully where he was placed. The chief jailer benefited from not having to worry; presumably the other prisoners gained from having a well-run prison and someone they could relate to in charge; but for Joseph there were no clear fiscal benefits. He did gain responsibility and probably a degree of freedom, but he remained a prisoner.

This begs the question of whether we are prepared to work faithfully when there are no clear benefits for us. We have choices in how we behave when the expected promotion or pay rise does not materialise, when our children do not thank us for hours of care, or when the charity that we volunteer for does not recognise our involvement. How do we cope when our actions go unnoticed? In our society, it is easy to think of success as that which is valued by others through an award, verbal praise or financial benefits. Yet Joseph's story questions whether our work can be successful even when it goes officially unrecognised and the credit is given to everyone else.

The ability to cope in these situations may indicate an even greater form of success – a mastery over one's emotions and reactions. Sacrificial living is not easy and does not fit within our usual terms of reference. Yet there are so many people whose service goes unnoticed. For me, one of these groups of unsung heroes are carers who year on year care for relatives who can no longer live without support. They may receive little or no financial benefit and yet their work is invaluable.

There is a danger in our busyness that we forget what it means to thank people, to hold a door open, to say a kind word or to smile. How we treat others is important.

Joseph's challenge is two fold. For those in positions of authority, there is the question of how we treat those who work for us. For those in support roles, there is the question of how we respond to our boss when we feel unrecognised and unvalued. For all of us, there is the question of what success really looks like.

At this stage in Joseph's story success was having a well-run prison. For us, success may be seen in fulfilling the objectives of the organisation that we work for. If success is less individualistic and more organisational, then this may change our perception of how we feel about our part in the broader picture.

Yet ultimately in Joseph's situation the success was God's. The ultimate goal was to work thoroughly and appropriately for the glory of God whatever the actual earthly benefits. In this way, Joseph lived out the principle outlined in Colossians:

> Work hard and cheerfully at whatever you do, as though you were working for the Lord rather than for people. Remember that the Lord will give you an inheritance as your reward, and the Master you are serving is Christ. (*Colossians* 3:23,24)

If this principle was applied to our daily life, what an impact it would have to the way we think and behave. It is so contrary to what our world says is important and yet it would free us to serve whether we are recognised or not.

The rewards for sacrificial living may not appear clear to us. Some of it may not make sense this side of eternity and some of the benefits will not appear till then. However, beneath the surface a depth of faith can be found when life is tough. It is forged in the darkness – but through the questions and confusion, recognition or silence, strength is found.

7 Downwards is upwards

(*Genesis* 40:1–22)

'Interpreting dreams is God's business,' Joseph
replied. 'Tell me what you saw' (*Genesis* 40:8).

JOSEPH MAY BE in prison but he has not lost the ability to be
compassionate. He has been assigned two new prisoners –
Pharaoh's chief cupbearer and chief baker, important men who
have fallen out of favour with Pharaoh. Joseph notices how
they respond and when he finds them particularly low one
day, he asks what the matter is and discovers that they have
had dreams that they don't understand. Joseph does not claim
any authority for himself but reminds them that it is God who
interprets dreams. Yet he does offer to listen and ends up ac-
curately interpreting what he hears.

All seven of us – my mum and dad, two brothers, sister and
sister-in-law – were away on a family holiday. My parents had
escaped to Israel a week earlier but the rest of us had just arrived. We had flown in at 6am and had already seen the remains at Caesarea and had swum in the sea. Now it was
evening. We were staying in a kibbutz and there was an area of

grass outside our rooms. So as the sun set, we sat out there chatting.

My dad often has problems with his teeth. While we talked, he bit into a nectarine. Suddenly his face changed expression and we knew something was wrong. It turned out that one of his front teeth had split in two. As he says, 'I looked like a vampire gone wrong!'[16] He wrapped the broken piece in a tissue and headed for the kibbutz reception.

The Jewish lady on reception found a dentist who could help, but when it came to directions, we had a real problem. Apparently it was not possible to explain the location to strangers because it was on one of the numerous back streets in Tiberias. She wrote a note in Hebrew requesting that anyone who read the note would assist the note bearer by pointing out the right direction. Her parting words were, 'Maybe someone will be kind!'[17]

I grabbed the car keys and we both jumped in the car to speed off to a destination yet unknown. As we set off, we prayed. Humanly, the whole scenario seemed ridiculous. There was no way we were going to find a dentist in the middle of an unknown city where we didn't know any of the language. It seemed typical that there was a disaster on the first day of us all being together!

As we drove into Tiberias, we stopped at traffic lights and showed two men the note and they pointed right but could say nothing in English. It was going to be a long trip! As we started up a steep hill, dad pointed out two more pedestrians so I pulled the car over. They were teenage lads. Dad asked if they spoke English and gave them the note. They knew where it was but quickly got stuck in trying to explain it. Eventually they suggested through a series of hand signals and pigeon English that they would come in the car and show us.

I wasn't sure what to make of this turn of events but as we

drove up hills, round corners and through a maze of rounda-
bouts and back streets it became clear – we never would have
found this place on our own! We ended up near a park and
outside the dentist's office. The two guys then got out the car.
They didn't want money, they just started walking back the
mile and a half to where we had found them walking in the
opposite direction!

As the boys wandered off down the hill, dad ran into the
dentist's while I parked the car. The dentist meticulously and
professionally sealed dad's tooth back together, and in a short
while we were returning to tell the others of the amazing kindness of two teenage lads and the expertise of a dentist who
had stayed late to help a foreigner. We were reminded at that
moment of the words of the lady on reception – maybe someone will be kind!

In a similar way, Joseph does not allow the situations that he
has been through to stop him from being kind. He may be lan-
guishing in prison but this does not stop him from seeing the
distress in the baker's and cupbearer's faces. He is able to see
the needs of others – how often do we? As human beings we
can be quick to judge each other and so fail to really see what
people are going through. We may see a wealthy person and
assume happiness, or a beggar and assume laziness. Yet what
lies behind the image that each of us projects?

Joseph stands before two men who have been very successful in terms of getting to be 'chief' of their profession. Joseph
may have been tempted to ignore them as he himself had
been forgotten, to feel inferior to them because of their previ-
ous position or to assume that they deserved their sudden
downfall – for why else would they be there? However, Joseph
does none of this. He notices when they appear to be particularly struggling. He sees the emotions that flicker over their

features and has the courage to reach out with compassion. He is kind.

Joseph's actions are a challenge to us. In our humanness, we create standards for judging success, but these very standards can blind us from seeing people as they are. Therefore if someone earns a certain amount, fits the image of a 'beautiful' person or has a great job, then we can assume that life is great for them. If life is not always great for us then why should it be for everyone else? Our assumptions can cause us to miss the signs that show us where people are struggling. All that we see is the image that they project, and we miss their human struggles and questions about life. We may not only do this to those that we assume are successful but also to those that we assume are not.

If our concept of success can blind us to the needs of others then maybe we should change our views? Character and compassion are also things that we can value as human beings. Is success about being people who can see the needs of others and reach out regardless of our own situation?

The film *Pay It Forward* demonstrates the impact that can be had if we look below the surface and seek to help others. Trevor is 11 and is starting Middle School. On the first day of class, the new teacher gives an unusual assignment: he challenges his pupils to do something to make the world a better place. Trevor has a difficult home situation, but takes the assignment seriously and devises a plan to help a tramp, his teacher and a bullied kid. He figures that if he can do something significant to help three people and they do something significant for three other people, then this will have a multiplying effect. This is a logical approach that has a powerful impact and significant consequences.

Trevor's age could have stopped him from reaching out to

others, but he did not let it. Joseph also did not allow prison from stopping him from demonstrating concern for other human beings. Do we allow our own situation or our view of other people to stop us from treating others as human beings needing love, respect and support? It can be as simple as trying to look at someone when we talk to them. To think about our questions so we mean what we ask. Then when we ask how someone is there is reality in the question.

Having said all this, is a concern for others enough to make someone successful? Is there not more to it than being 'huggy feely' people? Joseph did not only notice their obvious distress and offered to listen, he also announced God's role in the situation. It is God who interprets dreams, not humans. Sympathy and concern would not be enough to enable the baker and cupbearer to prepare for what would come next. They needed someone who could explain their dreams; they needed to meet a person who knew God well enough to be able to speak into their situation with some heavenly knowledge.

For the baker and cupbearer, their distress may be even more apparent in the light of their desire for understanding and clarity. In Pharaoh's palace they would have met the wise men and magicians – the very people Pharaoh would seek to interpret his dreams. In being thrown into prison, they were not only humiliated, but separated from the very people who could help them. They are now sharing their dreams with a young man – probably the last person they thought could give any insight. I wonder how hard it was for them to swallow their pride in order to accept Joseph's help.

The one person that they thought could not help them would be the one person who could because he knew the God who interprets dreams. Their disdain would turn to surprise and respect as Joseph both interprets the dreams and is proved to be accurate. There is a saying that a person can be 'so heavenly minded that they are of no earthly good', yet it is equally possible that we can be so earthly minded that we are of no heavenly use! Joseph needed to be heavenly minded to help the baker and cupbearer; compassion was not enough to give them understanding.

Stories are told of people who get talking to strangers about their faith in all kinds of locations. It would seem that train stations are a particular favourite! Personally, I don't find this a very easy thing to do and yet I am so grateful that I have brothers and sisters in Christ who do. Whether this is something we are comfortable with or not, there will be situations when God will want to speak into a context and we may be the only one around for him to use. The person we are talking to may not be a stranger, but there is a risk even in sharing with friends. Whatever people think of us, we have a choice: will we seek to hear God's voice in that situation or will we close our ears?

As Joseph said, interpretation is God's business but Joseph needed to be willing for God to use him. It is God who sees all things and knows all things, but Joseph was prepared to share what God revealed to him. When we are walking through our daily lives, are we ready for God to use us? In fact, are we asking him to speak through us both verbally and through our lifestyle? The challenge is to know God so much ourselves that we can hear his voice whether it is loud and clear or whether we just have a strong sense that this is what he is calling us to do. It is important to relate this to the God we know in the Bible so that it is not just our good intentions. Faith deepens as we read the Bible, as we seek to hear God during prayer times and as we listen to the way that God leads us through the Holy Spirit.

The situation with the baker and cupbearer comes 11 years after Joseph was first sold into slavery. He had had a lot of time to reflect. The Bible does not tell us what happened during this time in terms of Joseph's faith, but my guess is that it is in the silence of these years that Joseph's faith deepened. If it had not, he might have attempted to interpret the dreams on his own. His acknowledgement of God, suggests that he has been growing deeper in his knowledge and understanding of God.

In this encounter the baker and cupbearer discover that life is not as they assume it to be. People do not always fit stereotypes, and the one who successfully interprets their dreams is someone who they would have assumed to be very unsuccessful – he was a prisoner.

This dramatic reversal of expectations is not only relevant to the story of Joseph but is confirmed in the life and words of Jesus. God was prepared to come down to earth, to be born in poor and pitiful circumstances as the baby Jesus so that one day he could draw all people to himself (John 12:32). Jesus also challenged his disciples when they argued among themselves about who was the greatest, that those who want to be great need to be servants of all. He later demonstrated that his is an 'upside-down kingdom'[18] by taking the role of a slave and washing their feet.

Jesus reveals that the kingdom he came to build does not function in the way our earthly societies do. Power in the kingdom of God is not gained by trampling on other people's heads in the rush up the ladder of society, but by going downwards to serve others. For those of us who claim to follow Jesus, there is the challenge not to skim over his words as we read the Gospels but to take seriously their challenge and live by a different set of values.

In our churches we use the expression 'servant leadership', but how many of us know what this looks like? For a year and a half, my role at church was to coordinate setting up. We meet in a school so everything has to be packed and unpacked from a cupboard each Sunday. Then the chairs need to be neatly arranged. I did the job but certainly did not revel in it. I struggled with a role that I knew was essential, but did not really want to do. Yet I learned a lot in that time – not only about the way other people treat you, but also about my own pride and assumptions about myself.

It is not enough simply to know the words that Christians profess. We need to know the God – Father, Son and Holy Spirit – that Christians seek to follow. If God's Kingdom lasts forever, and downwards in service is really upwards in living as God intended, questions must be asked about our priorities. Whatever our position, we need to be careful not to lord it over others. To trample on them in our desperation to gain earthly success is not only wrong but, in the long term, pointless. This is not to say that earthly success should be rejected by Christians. However, there are questions about how we view success and the degree to which we revel in our own achievement rather than seeking to glorify God by the way we live.

There is a danger that in rejecting the world's definitions of success we may cut ourselves off from those around us. Separation does not enable us to obey the words of Jesus – to share what we have discovered with others. No, the challenge is to live in a world that seems so important but whose values are upside down compared to those of the kingdom that we are waiting for. If we don't want to follow God here on earth, why should we want to know him for eternity?

It is not enough to spend our lives relying on people simply to be kind. If Joseph had only offered sympathy, he would have left the baker and cupbearer with three days of confusion and despair (although the news for the baker may not

74

have helped much!). God knows what it is to live in reverse. Jesus demonstrated on earth that downwards is upwards. If we claim to follow him, how dare we live any other way?

8   Frustrated?

(*Genesis* 40:23, 41:1)

'The chief cupbearer, however, did not remember
Joseph; he forgot him. When two full years had
passed...'(*Genesis* 40:23; 41:1, NIV).

JOSEPH HAD PLAYED the ultimate 'get out of jail' card. He had
helped the *chief* cupbearer, a man close to Pharaoh who could
put in a good word for him. Surely now Joseph would be freed.
Now things would change.

<hr>

Anna is a capable woman with lots of dreams, passion and
laughter. Her family are from the Caribbean but she grew up in
London. As a child, her parents regularly said to her, 'You've
got to be better than average and if you're the best, you'll succeed.' She was never quite sure whether this was because of
the colour of her skin or if parents generally say this.

She worked for a number of years but did evening classes
and kept learning. Soon she was the first member of her family
to go to university. She had a great time, worked hard and did
well. She looked like she was heading for the promised
success.

Then one day she applied for a job as the office manager in

a large company. In many ways, this was her dream job. The recruitment agency and others had said that she was the best person for the job. It was down to the last two candidates and she secretly expected to get it. However the interviewer had a different perspective. His conclusion was something like this, 'You are clearly the better one for the job and I see that you've got a lot to offer. But I'm not going to give the job to you. I'm going to give it to the other girl because she's the safer option.'

Anna was shocked. Everyone was wrong, even her parents. She turned to her mum and said, 'You said if I was the best, I would succeed. But I was the best and I didn't succeed!'[19]

I wonder whether Joseph felt similarly about his situation. He had faithfully served others both as a servant and now as a prisoner. He would have done countless menial tasks. Finally there is some hope for a better future on the horizon. However, the reality of life just wasn't meeting Joseph's expectations. He had sought to help others and had trusted that they would want to also help him. Success for the chief cupbearer was getting out of prison; success for Joseph could be seen as the same thing. The chief cupbearer's forgetfulness demonstrates an apparent fickleness. He got what he wanted from Joseph but when he no longer needed him he forgot Joseph's request.

However, the chief cupbearer probably viewed this moment in a very different light. He had been thrown into prison, his life had flashed before him, and now all that is past and he is restored to his original position. No wonder he didn't want to remember the past. He may also have been fearful of arousing Pharaoh's anger, and so forgetting Joseph was simply a sensible move on his part. It meant he could continue as before and work on ways of currying favour with Pharaoh. Joseph was only a prisoner and therefore was not important enough to help him progress in his career or social standing. The chief cupbearer's forgetfulness could have been a tactical move to ensure his social and political survival.

The connection between times of struggle and forgetfulness may also impact us. It is so easy to forget those that help us grow. So often those experiences that enable us to develop, come in times of difficulties and there is an attempt to forget them. Struggle and challenges can feel like a blip on our horizon. We may be tempted to think that they should not be part of our experience and so paint over the pain with the whitewash of forgetfulness.

Those memories of painful periods of life are brushed aside and so we affirm all of our illusions that pain and struggle should not be part of our existence. We chase the latest illusion of grandeur – all those elements of wealth, prestige and human accolade that we think will make us significant. We cover up anything that would question that these things are not the most important. We forget that our memories and history are all part of making us who we are. We put our energies into the future. But are there things in our history that still need to be dealt with? Are we closing the door on unfinished business?

Joseph had been sold into slavery at the age of 17 (Genesis 37:2) and he would have to wait until he was 30 to be released from prison (Genesis 41:46). At this stage Joseph had been a servant or prisoner for over ten years. He was 28, single, and unable to control the direction of his life.

In asking the chief cupbearer to remember him, was Joseph trying to fix things? It may have been a casual comment. Joseph might have seen this as the way that God would deliver him. Alternatively, Joseph may have tried consciously or subconsciously to manipulate his connections in order to improve his situation. There is no indication that Joseph was struggling with prison or a sense of urgency to do something useful with his life, and yet his clear leadership abilities may suggest that he got frustrated with the limitations placed upon him.

The question of Joseph's intentions is a question as to how we live. When life is confusing or challenging, it is tempting to seek to 'fix' things. For some reason, pain, suffering and struggle are not on our radar. We try to solve things quickly and move on. One way to fix things is to reach for more constantly. If we are not being acknowledged then we may grasp for success in terms of power, authority, position, and prestige in order to justify our existence somehow. Yet Joseph had to learn to wait for God's timing.

Waiting is far from fashionable in our instant society of microwave meals, one minute loans, and unlimited broadband. In all the speed of today, it is unsurprising that periods of waiting hit us with a sense of failure. Interestingly, Jesus had to wait until he was about 30 to start his ministry. Thirty is not a magic age when all good things happen (or at least that's what they tell me!). It is just that there is a maturity and deepening of understanding and insight that can happen with waiting that means there is more to draw upon and offer others when life gets busy again.

At 28, Joseph had thought he had solved his problems with a friendly request, but it would not be until he was 30 that he would be ready for service as the second-in-command of the nation. If he had expected a logical progression from prison to second-in-command, he was in for a rude surprise. Joseph would be thrown directly from one to the other. He would need to learn in prison what would be required to help lead a nation. It is easy to look down on our current situations as irrelevant for all that will come next but there is value in today as it will be part of all that tomorrow will be.

When I was about 16, I used to meet with a woman in our

church to pray and read the Bible. She was a mum with three young children and was very artistic. I loved talking to Trinny because we had such different perspectives on life and I had so much to learn from her. One day, Trinny said to me, 'Vicky, you know what your problem is?' [I thought, 'No, but you're about to tell me!']. She said, 'You look at life like a tunnel. If you get through your A-levels and then university, you will finally enter into all that God has for you. But life is not like that. Life is like a jigsaw. Every stage of life is a piece of the jigsaw. Together it makes up the whole picture.'[20]

I am having to learn to have patience with the pieces. I still want a sneak preview of the jigsaw box's lid so I can see the whole picture! The challenge I find is continuing to value the different stages of life and learn all that I can so that I will be ready for the next piece.

Likewise, prison for Joseph was a piece of the jigsaw. The waiting probably made no sense to him. Why was it necessary? We don't know. It may have been for Joseph to grow in maturity and understanding, or because Pharaoh wasn't yet in a position to relate to Joseph or need a second-in-command. Whether it was for external or internal reasons, or even no apparent reason, it is largely irrelevant because it is what happened. The issue was how Joseph would deal with the silence of these two years.

The Bible emphasises the deafening nature of this silence by referring to it in two different ways. It is said both that the chief cupbearer *did not remember* and that *he forgot* Joseph (40:23, NIV). There is no other explanation, no other comment about what this meant to Joseph or the impact it had on his emotions or situation. And yet, here is a young man who had dreamed of leadership and authority still wondering if he would ever know the freedom of release.

In imagining Joseph in the dark, forgotten and alone, I can

almost hear him yell, 'You said people would bow down to me, you said I would lead, what am I still doing here?!' It may be that life seems to have fitted together for us, but for many the frustration and anger of unfulfilled expectations is real and painful.

In the struggle, there are questions. Where is God in the apparent silence of prison, unemployment, broken relationships and damaged dreams? Unlike earlier parts of Joseph's story, there is no narrator to tell us that, 'God was with Joseph,' and yet I believe he was. In a similar way, God is with us even when we can't sense it. When there is nothing else to cling to, do we trust that he is there regardless of how we feel? When life seems to be going well, we talk more easily about God's presence. But God does not go on holiday the moment life gets difficult. Our friends may be that fickle, but the creator of the universe is not frightened away by pain.

It is we human beings, especially in wealthier nations, who appear to do all we can to numb ourselves or hide from suffering. We may seek to dull our senses or freeze our emotions through addictive involvement in sport, watching endless television programmes, getting drunk, taking drugs or doing a variety of other activities. Avoidance does not 'fix' pain; it simply puts it on hold.

When I lived in the States, I read a book on bereavement by a man whose wife had died. He spoke of the need to 'face the darkness'. As he came to face the reality of his wife's loss, he somehow found the courage to keep living. The 'darkness' that we want to run from is hard to face and yet there is something that we can learn and become through facing our fears and confusion.

Brother Yun is a Christian from China who faced persecution and imprisonment at the hands of the authorities. He describes his experiences in his book, *The Heavenly Man*, and he challenges the way we are tempted to think about suffering:

> How we mature as Christians largely depends on the attitude we have when we're faced with suffering. Some try to avoid it or imagine it doesn't exist, but that will only make the situation worse. Others try to endure grimly hoping for relief. This is better but falls short of the full victory God wants to give each of his children. The Lord wants us to embrace suffering as a friend.[21]

The problem with pain avoidance and with grim determination is that they stop us from seeing beneath the situation. We are either so caught up in trying to ignore our circumstances, or so focused on getting through them, that we miss any lessons that can be learned from them. We block our ears from hearing because we are convinced no good can come from it. If we could only stop reacting and start listening, we may discover that God has so been there all along and has much to teach us.

There are many of us who would struggle to call suffering a 'friend' and yet there is something that can be discovered through suffering that would not be found otherwise. In life, we so often rely on our own energies and experience to get us through, yet in suffering we face the limits of our human strength, understanding and abilities. We face the depth of who we are. Who do we really trust when nothing else makes sense?

The hope found in darkness has more resilience than the assurance of constantly fulfilled wants and expectations. This depth has a price but there is value in the treasure produced. Like sand in a shell, eventually a pearl will be created.

9 Stored strength

(*Genesis* 41:1–36)

'Have them gather all the food and grain of these good years into the royal storehouses, and store it away ... That way there will be enough to eat when the seven years of famine come' (*Genesis* 41:35, ,36).

AFTER TWO YEARS of being forgotten, Joseph's life suddenly goes from rags to riches. In the crisis created by Pharaoh's dream, and through the words of the cupbearer, Joseph is suddenly rushed into the presence of the king as the only one in the land who can interpret the dream. He quickly sets the record straight: 'I cannot do it ... but God will give Pharaoh the answer he desires' (Genesis 41:16, NIV).

Cheryl is 42. She's one of those people who can always make you smile and often make you laugh out loud. She loves kids and always wanted to be a full-time itinerant Christian children's worker. She started studying for this but her health began to fail.

When she was 30, she became chronically ill and has never recovered; in fact things are getting worse. She currently has chronic constructive pulmonary disease (which affects her heart and lungs), brittle asthma and emphysema. She is constantly on oxygen through her nose and is regularly in hospital. It would be easy for her to blame God but she doesn't.

She had faith before her illness and is determined to keep growing in her knowledge of God despite it. Her ambition is 'dying with my boots on'. She has led over 100 people to faith in Jesus because she is willing to see the needs and respond. It is rare that she starts the conversation but when she leaves her home, she asks God to use her that day. She is adamant that it is 'not me, it never has been ... I couldn't do any of it without him [God].' Yet she is open. She has people stopping in the street to talk to her and as one lady said, 'You just look like someone who has some answers.'

Her willingness to pray and be used by God is an example. It is not exclusive to these years of struggle; it is part of who she is. 'Because God gives me a reason for living, to talk about him, that gives me a reason to keep living. I couldn't let go of God, even if I tried. Where else am I going to go, who else am I going to go to?'[22]

The challenge in talking to Cheryl is knowing that there has been no full stop. She had faith before the illness and she has faith now. There have been questions and struggles. Yet in the years of good health she trusted God and now in these years of pain she continues to do the same.

This attitude is reflected in Joseph's response to Pharaoh. He not only interprets the dreams but proposes a solution. He explains that the harvest will be abundant for seven years and then there will be seven years of famine. The memories of the good years will potentially be lost in the pain of the bad ones, as the thin cows swallow the fat ones and the withered heads of stalk consume the plump ones (Genesis 41:2–7). Therefore, he suggests that the reserves from the good years are preserved for the sake of the tough ones. There needs to be a flow from one to the other even though the circumstances are different.

Joseph took a risk. He was still a prisoner when he dared to suggest a plan to Pharaoh. Joseph realised that it was not enough to understand the dream. The real challenge was to decide what to do with that knowledge. He was not prepared to see the dreams fulfilled without exploring a way to change the ending.

Interestingly, Joseph does not respond to the dream by praying that God would stop the famine. Immediately he recognised that 'having the dreams twice … means that the matter has been decreed by God' (Genesis 41:32), yet he was not prepared to accept that this should cause the death of all the people. The famine would come, but Pharaoh's actions on Joseph's suggestion could impact the outcome.

It may be that we are living in the good years. Life seems to be working out for us and our dreams are being fulfilled. This is great. There is nothing to feel guilty about; but there is the question of how we are using the strength of these years. Each of us will face more difficult times in life. It is not something to fret about. But how we grow and learn in the good times will affect what strength we have to draw on in the tough ones.

It would have been so easy for the Egyptians to waste the grain in the seven abundant years, but they stored it instead. It may be that we need to think through how we use all the good things that we have. It is not necessarily about saving money or gathering possessions. For Cheryl, it has been developing a deep faith so that there was spiritual strength to draw on when life became difficult.

We do not store things up so that we can admire all that has been horded or so we can cope in difficult times, but so that we can continue to serve God. Cheryl needed the spiritual strength not only to endure her current suffering, but so that she could continue to live out her faith to those around her.

Her example can make us feel uncomfortable, but her story also contains a challenge. When I was growing up, I felt like people measured their success as a Christian by how many people they had led through the 'sinner's prayer'. I always felt like such a failure for not having a checklist of converts! I talk to Cheryl and am reminded that it is not about guilt. We can allow this emotion to stop us from doing anything but that would not honour God. What God wants is for us to be open and expectant so that he can use us to reach out to others.

Trees and skyscrapers have something in common: they have deep foundations. The roots of a tree need to go deep and wide in order to support the parts that we see above ground. The same is true for the foundations of skyscrapers. If the roots or the foundations are not deep enough then the tree or the skyscraper will not stay upright during a storm. The challenge is the same for us. Are we digging deep foundations in the good times that will enable us to stand whatever pressures we may face?

As Christians, the foundations deepen as we seek to grow in faith. There are times when this happens easily and naturally. There are other times when it takes sheer determination and effort. We read our Bible because we trust that God will teach us through it, even when we don't feel like we are learning anything. Or we pray because we want to hear God, even if we are not sure he's speaking. It is as we invest time and energy in developing our relationship with God that the foundations will deepen.

It takes time to store and it takes time to implement dreams. For Joseph, the two came together in the same activity. However, Joseph did not announce that the famine was coming, and instantly food was produced. He had to agree a response, organise the people, arrange for adequate storehouses to be available etc. It required a business proposal to Pharaoh and a set of action plans.

Similarly, we may have big dreams but if we have not thought about the steps necessary to fulfil them we may never attain them. Many a vision is lost in the mundane activity of life because people have not thought through how to put it into action. It may be that you dreamed of serving God and so changing your world for Jesus but that this has been lost under the bills and pressures of life. It may be that now is the time to re-examine those dreams.

The dreams of childhood need not be discarded in the reality of adulthood. We need to know where God is leading us. It may be that the dreams were self-centred and it is right that they have been pushed aside. However, we may equally have become trapped in the busyness of today that we have lost a vision for tomorrow.

Joseph knew that to save the people through seven years of famine needed preparation and commitment. We live in a society that expects everything instantly. It is unlikely that our dreams can be fulfilled that way. We need to learn how to store up strength in the good times to be better prepared for the tough ones. We also need to know how to plan and act over time to see our dreams fulfilled. The temptation is to waste what we have; yet at what cost for the future?

10 Fame and Faithfulness

(*Genesis* 41:37–52)

Can we find anyone like this man, one in whom is the spirit of God (*Genesis* 41:38, NIV)?

SUDDENLY, AT THE age of 30, Joseph is catapulted from prison to the palace. He is now second-in-command to Pharaoh. He is given symbols of his new position: a ring, fine robes, a gold chain, a chariot, a new name, and an Egyptian wife. In the years of abundance, he has two sons – Manasseh and Ephraim. Things are now looking up – Joseph is the second most powerful man in the land; he is a celebrity!

As the room quietens, 140 engineers turn their attention to the next presenter. Chris stands up. He is in his early thirties and probably the only non-engineer in the room but he is here to do a job. With positive assurance he starts to speak.

At this moment life is the best it has ever been for Chris. But it was not always like this.

Chris and I were friends at university, where we both read theology. After university, he headed to his parents' home where he spent a frustrating year looking for work, despite having an MA. Eventually he was offered a good job in

London. So he packed his bags and headed south full of hope and expectation.

But it wasn't long before his world came crashing down. Within weeks he had a head injury and was off work for three and a half months. This was almost immediately followed by a burst appendix and another two and a half months off work. He got back to the office as soon as he could but it was too much. He suffered a nervous breakdown and was diagnosed with depression. Finally he resigned from his job.

Now he was not working he had a lot of time to himself. Amidst the pain and confusion, he started self-harming simply to decrease his anxiety. Life was feeling overwhelming. Just when he thought it couldn't get any worse, he was attacked by someone he trusted. None of it made any sense.

In the space of a year he had gone from the jubilation of a new future to the depths of despair in the agony of his present. However, it was not to end here. He went into therapy and with time started to do some part-time temporary work before getting a low-level permanent job. He also met the woman of his dreams who agreed to become his wife.

Things were looking up, but not for long. The company he was with was struggling financially, so he left. But he had difficulties finding another job. His home situation changed so now he was temporarily house-sitting. Then, Chris suffered a depressive relapse. All of this caused much concern to his prospective in-laws!

However, his beautiful fiancée stood by him and in time they married and found somewhere more permanent to live. Almost five years after leaving university, Chris began a temping job with an engineering-based company. It is a strange place for a theologian to find his feet but he was soon given a permanent position and 18 months later promoted internally. Now he is the youngest manager in the company. As he says, 'I am still an introverted, melancholic person by nature. But this is not irreconcilable with overflowing joy.'[23] The years of pain may still not make much sense but he found hope in the midst of it:

> No matter how bad it seems life gets, God is faithful and will not abandon you. When I was at my lowest point after serious illness and a nervous breakdown, the only thing that kept me going was looking at the night sky and gazing at all the stars and seeing God's hand holding the universe in place. This consolation enabled me to struggle through the darkest nights and the loneliest moments. We don't always understand why things happened – look at Job – but God is still faithful; we need to grasp a hold of him, and not let go.[24]

The stars would remind him that on the 'black canvas of life there are pinpricks of hope'.[25]

And today, in all the joy of life he concludes that 'as cruel as it may sound, God's grace allowed me to go through those times – my experiences and the way I have wrestled with them have made me who I am today, more complete that I would otherwise have been.'[26]

Like Chris, Joseph's life seems to have been a rollercoaster ride. He has experienced years of darkness, and now suddenly at 30 he is catapulted into recognition. It would be easy to look at Joseph's situation and say, 'After all he went through, he deserved it. It was about time something good happened to him.' Yet Scripture says nothing about 'deserving'. God allows Joseph to be in this position for a purpose – to save his people from starvation. Joseph's suffering did not earn him earthly honour. God allowed it for his purposes. Joseph also had a choice. He could get a big head or he could faithfully serve.

Scripture tells us what Joseph did but it doesn't tell us what he thought about it. I wonder how he felt about the sudden transformation. It was probably tempting for Joseph to start to believe his own publicity and so get an inflated ego. He had spent years faithfully working in secret; now the lessons learned there would be tested in the fires of apparent human success. Would he be able to hold on to an accurate perception of himself while living up to all the responsibility and opportunity that this new position would entail?

In A *Knight's Tale*, Heath Ledger plays a servant, William Thatcher, who pretends to be a knight after the death of his master so as to enter jousting competitions to survive. In the end, his deception is discovered and he is put in the stocks. As everyone gathers around to humiliate him, his friends draw near to defend him. At that moment, the prince who has been hiding in the crowd comes forward to save him. He declares that William is from an ancient aristocratic family line and then shocks everyone by knighting him. One second William faced disgrace and public humiliation, the next he is honoured and publicly affirmed. As the crowd watch in surprise, disbelief and pleasure fight each other across William's face.

In a similar way, Joseph's fortunes are reversed in seconds. He had spent 13 years as a slave or a prisoner; now he is suddenly the equivalent of Prime Minister. Yet like William, Joseph knew he hadn't suddenly become a different person. Although he was the same person, people's perceptions of him and of his importance changed in an instant. The knowledge that nothing had changed and yet everything had, probably seemed strange; did this new-found success feel like an illusion?

An illusion is something transitory; it has no substance. The experience of fame may feel real but its potentially fleeting nature challenges our assumptions about its value. People's attitudes can change very quickly and, as various celebrities demonstrate, money can be lost or spent as easily as it is gained. Therefore there is a danger in viewing ourselves only through the eyes of others as measured by our possessions and other people's praise.

If our business goes bust, we are made redundant, unemployed or retire, our self-worth can be damaged because the work that gave us value in the eyes of others, and even ourselves, is gone. Surely we are created to have worth beyond the flimsy perception of ourselves and others towards our earthly achievements? Therefore we need to guard ourselves against believing our own publicity. Otherwise we will be defined by our illusions of grandeur and so miss out on our intrinsic value as human beings.

In Genesis 1 we read how God created human beings and breathed life into them. In sending Jesus to earth, God demonstrated how much he loves us and wants us to know him. We each have value as people created and loved by God and we each have gifts and abilities. Some of these are more obvious than others but that does not undermine the fact that each person is significant and has something to contribute to the community. If we could see ourselves as valuable and loved by God, would it change the way we often view ourselves?

Our image of ourselves can often be impacted by what other people say, and also by what we choose to believe about ourselves. In undermining our gifts and abilities, we also are in danger of undermining the giver of those gifts and abilities. The opposite challenge is to so exult in our gifts that we become proud and look down on other people and devalue the significance of the giver. Both positions are wrong but we so easily fall into one or the other. The real challenge is to view ourselves as loved by God with gifts and abilities that need to be used for his glory but also to recognise that we are not the answer to all the world's ills – God is!

Humility is not about looking down on ourselves but recognising our limitations while valuing our gifts and seeking to serve God and others where we are. This can be a real challenge if fame or great opportunities present themselves to us. If we could only glimpse more of how God views us and less of how we and other people view us, then we would be much better off! For God sees all people and so knows the limits of each of us individually and yet he loves each of us enough to want us to know him ourselves.

If we are seeking after God and we end up in a position of authority then this leads to the question of what it means to live as a Christian. If faith is more than outward activity, surely it must impact the way we view ourselves and how we live our lives. Joseph is called 'one in whom is the spirit of God' (v 38, NIV). What does it mean to be people in whom the Spirit of God dwells? If the Holy Spirit dwells in our lives then is this seen by those around us?

Part of the issue is bringing our faith and our lifestyle in line with each other. For too many years there has been a tendency to divide people's private and public life and to say that faith should only impact the private. But we are whole people and so our faith should impact every area of our lives, otherwise we are no better than hypocrites. It is tempting to live up to the expectations of others. Even in Christian circles, there can be expectations of how a 'successful person' should live. It often serves to mirror more of the self-serving elements of the American dream than to demonstrate a life of sacrifice.

We are human and crave the security of many things, including good food, nice clothes, and a comfortable home. In themselves, these things are not necessarily wrong but are markers of the good life, and as such are only temporary. Yet while we enjoy such luxuries much of the world is starving to death. We may feel we deserve these things because that's what other people in our position have, but do we really need them?

In these ways, we perpetuate the myths of what's important simply by how we live. We are role models to those who follow us and we help affirm the criteria of what is appropriate. I am not suggesting that we reject everything that seems worldly – Joseph accepted the wife, position, ring and other honours. What we need is to think about what we are doing and what our life is saying about our faith!

This does not mean we confine our lives to what we consider to be religious activity. Jesus knew what it meant to engage with people where they are. He began his ministry not in a place of religious worship but at a wedding. And the first miracle recorded in John's Gospel is not a healing but turning water into wine (John 2). Sometimes we get so caught up with what image we are portraying of our faith that we lose sight of what it means to live our faith before others.

So, whether we are living in the depths of despair or the joy of new opportunities, God is there and he sees how we live. If we lived like we believed he was watching our every move, would we still get caught up with a desire for fame and our rights to have certain things? There is a tension between our pronouncements about God's faithfulness and our willingness to trust him, and the way we often rely more on our own ability to provide for ourselves. Are we missing what it really means to live authentically?

11 Beyond ourselves

(*Genesis* 41:53–57)

…Joseph opened up the storehouses…(*Genesis* 41:56).

JOSEPH'S LIFE IS turned around after interpreting Pharaoh's dream. However, he is wise and in the good years he stores enough grain that when the years of famine come, there is enough to feed those living in Egypt and beyond. Therefore, when the people cry out to Pharaoh for help, he simply tells them to talk to Joseph. And Joseph opens the storehouses.

From the main road, the sun reflecting off tin roofs makes the vast area look like a field of shiny silver. But the glint masks one of the largest slums in Kenya. It is here that thousands live with no running water, electricity or sanitation.

Martha and her husband are Kenyans who studied in the USA. When they returned to Kenya everyone expected them to get good jobs and earn lots of money. They were supposed to find a nice house and settle down with their two little boys. But they shocked their relatives by announcing that they felt God calling them to start a church in this slum.

When I went to visit Kenya, Martha invited Tina, my former

flatmate, and me to see the church. Tina is Kenyan, in her twenties and a professional with little experience of the slum. We met Martha at the road and unsurprisingly she led the way to the church.

The slum is a sprawling mass of mud walls and tin roofs, open sewers, bleating goats and children yelling at me, 'How are you?' The route was like an obstacle course. We walked tentatively over a bridge that resembled a wooden ladder. Next we clung to a gate while manoeuvring over a pool of dirty water. Lastly, we had to grip on to the side of a mud wall and gingerly put our feet on small stones so as to avoid the bog of sewage and mud. I say gingerly – Martha's agility made that task look easy!

As the foreigner I was determined not to look pathetic. I had survived this far and would continue to do so. I made an effort to look like I knew what I was doing! I clung to the wall while trying to project an air of relaxed confidence. Tina was following me. As I was half way across, Tina suddenly spoke up, 'The reason why I don't do this is I have a small heart.'[27]

Her honesty humbled and challenged me. She was the local, I the foreigner. I was trying to put on a good show, yet she was open about her struggles. She was vulnerable while I was not. Her actions reminded me of how tempting it can be to act as if we are the ones who are superior rather than have the courage to admit our weakness.

Those of us who claim to be Christians can face this challenge in how we talk about our faith. We know that we are saved through Christ's death and resurrection and we need to have the courage to share this with our friends. But if we talk about Jesus with an air of superiority, we miss the point. There was a time in each of our lives when we did not know God for ourselves and even now we know that there is so much more to discover. Our arrogance can stop others from discovering

God for themselves because they cannot see beyond what we portray.

It is this same attitude that can close our hearts from the needs around us. The pain may be too deep, the issues too large and the questions too sharp. So we protect ourselves, intentionally or not. Like Tina, we need to admit our weakness. We need to be willing to be vulnerable and stop acting as if we can do everything ourselves. We need God to open our hearts.

Joseph's heart was open and he was willing to respond. The famine would last for seven years and the passage shows how serious the situation was in the number of references to all the people who were affected. When the people came from Pharaoh to Joseph for help, it would have been easy for Joseph to tell them that the situation wasn't really serious: 'Go home and come back when it's *really* bad.' Yet Joseph doesn't; he responds to their needs and opens the storehouses. It would be interesting to get an insider's look at Joseph's feelings and actions at this moment but the passage doesn't tell us. Given his position, it is unlikely that he was suffering from hunger yet he was still compassionate and opened the way for people to access food the moment they genuinely needed it.

In our world, we can see needs all the time displayed on our TV screens. Usually they are not our needs, and often they appear so extreme or so distant from our situation that it is easy to become immune to them. Suffering and pain are not things that we like to think about and for some reason are not something we expect. When people do face pain, the response is often, 'Why me?' If we can't comprehend the pain of others, surely it will be very difficult for us to see needs and respond? In this way, it is difficult for us to follow Joseph's example.

Looking beyond ourselves is more than just about what we

see; it is about how we use what we have. It is about steward-ship. Joseph used the knowledge that God had given him from Pharaoh's dream, and his position as the second most influen-tial person in the land, to enable him to store up resources so that people would not starve during the years of drought. He did not allow wealth and recognition to stop him from interact-ing with those in need or to lead him into corruption. He sold the grain but he did not limit it to the ruling family. He could have restricted the grain to certain people, or Egyptians only, so as to win friends and influence people, but he did not. His diligence during the good years eased the suffering of many during the hard years and his honesty meant that everyone survived.

Whether in prison or as an influential leader, Joseph re-sponded to the needs of others and was trusted by those in leadership over him. Pharaoh's apparent respect is shown in his response to the people, 'Go to Joseph and do whatever he tells you' (Genesis 41:55). There is something greater than success in terms of material possessions, and it is linked with using what we have wisely. Joseph was trusted because he had shown himself as someone who could be responsible with what he had been given.

Wealth, fame and praise are very popular in our culture. Re-ality TV highlights how many people are craving those sec-onds of fame and magazines honour those people who achieve it. Steve Kaufman, an American artist who has drawn the likes of Princess Diana, Marilyn Monroe and Frank Sinatra, suggests that there is a distinction among those who are fa-mous, dependent on how they use their fame and whether they respond to the needs of others:

There's a difference between the celebrities and the icons. I mean Frank Sinatra is an icon, Princess Diana is an icon. What I mean by icon is, a person who reaches beyond their realm and helps people.[28]

Kaufman's distinction is helpful in thinking about different levels of success: one appears self-orientated, the other sacrificial. The latter is illustrated by Sir Bob Geldof, who used his position, time and energy to organise the Live Aid and Live 8 concerts in order to highlight issues of poverty and be a voice for those that may not otherwise have a voice. Such people have a chance of being good stewards because of how they use their influence for the benefit of others.

It is not just celebrities that have a chance to live differently. In our contexts, the same question needs answering: *what are we doing with what we have been given*?

In all of this – both the seeing and the doing – there is an element of choice. There is the chance to stand for something that really counts, to say, 'I choose to live differently, not necessarily by leaving my environment but by seeking to live beyond myself by seeing the needs of others.'

Such people may appear to be exceptional, but what makes them exceptional is their choice to stand for principles that are beyond personal fame or need. This is illustrated by the psychologist Viktor Frankl, who survived life in a concentration camp under the Nazis during World War II:

> We who lived in concentration camps can remember the men who walked through the huts comforting others, giving away their last piece of bread. They may have been few in number, but they offer sufficient proof that everything can be taken from a man but one thing: the last of the human freedoms – to choose one's attitude in any given set of circumstances, to choose one's own way.[29]

It is tempting to feel swept along with the tide of life but there is still a choice, whatever our circumstances, to have an attitude that is for others and not just me. To seek first God's kingdom and not our own praise. This is much easier said than done, but what an example we could be!

Joseph also had a choice – to obey God or not. The scholar Victor Hamilton describes Joseph as 'an antitype of Noah, building storehouses just as Noah built his ark. The storehouses of Joseph, however, are for the survival of the masses. The ark of Noah was for the survival of one man and his family.'[30] The difficulty with making parallels between stories is that too much is assumed. The Bible tells us a lot about what Noah's neighbours thought of him building the ark but the Bible tells us nothing of what the Egyptians thought of Joseph's storehouses. Yet both did what they did because they believed what God had revealed to them either directly or through a dream.

I can imagine people teasing Joseph for storing too much. 'Hey Joseph, surely there's enough now – the grain's like sand' (Genesis 41:49)! 'There's being prepared and then there's being ridiculous.' 'What if you're wrong, what will we do with all this food?' He chose to trust God, even though it took years to prove that he was right!

It is easy to think of such people as exceptional, but if each one of us allowed God to open our eyes and hearts, what impact would be made? It is not about a particular formula for doing things but about allowing God to transform us into his image and enable us to see beyond our own needs. It is so easy to be overwhelmed by all the pressures of life. We may feel busy, exhausted and struggling with our own issues – are there things that we could/should stop doing? It is easy to talk about having a relationship with God but do we create space to listen to God's direction in our lives? Are we willing to allow God to touch our hearts and make us uncomfortable? Are we too busy chasing our own comfort to look beyond ourselves? I find these questions uncomfortable but if we don't ask them will we really be all that we were created to be?

The people in this chapter are worthy of note because of their example. But this does not mean we can put them on a pedestal and so excuse ourselves for our inaction. Instead we must accept the challenge to live our ordinary lives exceptionally.

Some of the people I respect most are seeking to follow Jesus' example in their everyday lives. They may not be well known, but God sees the way that they are completely sold out for him. It is the carer whose constant love for their sick or elderly relative speaks volumes of God's love. It is the time given by many busy people through voluntary work that speaks of a compassion for others. It is in the words of someone sharing openly about their faith. The danger is that this can all sound like more actions, more things to do. But it is about allowing God to use us. It is about being willing to have our hearts enlarged.

12 Family Matters

(*Genesis* 42:1 – 45:3)

'I am Joseph!' he said to his brothers.
'Is my father still alive?'
But his brothers were speechless (*Genesis* 45:3).

WHAT A SHOCK for Joseph's brothers. They must have wondered about this powerful man whose behaviour seemed so erratic. One day he accuses them of being spies and throws them into prison; the next he gives them grain and returns their money. But he warns them that they can buy no more grain until they return with their brother Benjamin and prove that they are who they say they are.

However, when they take Benjamin (after a lot of promises to their father) they are honoured with a meal and then accused of stealing. When the silver cup is found in Benjamin's bag he is threatened with slavery and Judah steps in to defend him by offering himself. Eventually Joseph can keep up the charade no longer. He breaks down and reveals who he is. His brothers are stunned into silence. The dreams were true – they have already bowed down to this man, their brother.

———⋅•⊙•⋅———

It was a beautiful, sunny day in the South of France. I was a teenager on the annual family holiday. We had escaped the busyness of London life. In the UK, my dad was involved in national Christian leadership. In certain circles he was quite well known, but here in France we were anonymous. It was great just to be a family and not have lots of other people wanting his attention. It was so good to be 'normal', to relax, play games and swim with nothing else to think about.

On the campsite there was a kids' club. Suzy, the youngest, had spent the morning there. The rest of us were lounging around the tent, reading or chatting. Dad had got up to start getting some food ready. At that moment, the kids' club leader turned up with Suzy in tow. As she looked at our domestic bliss, she suddenly recognised my dad. She had been to Spring Harvest, an annual UK Christian event which my dad co-founded and where both my parents were on the speakers' team. In her surprise, she said, 'I can't believe it, you're so famous!'

This incident has become a bit of a family joke. Our dad is our dad. I am grateful for his example and the ways that God has used him but he is very human. The problem with people who are well-known is that we can lose sight of the person and only see the image that we have created of who they are. This is what Joseph's brothers seem to have done. They meet this powerful man in Egypt and all they can see is his wealth and status. Admittedly it's been a long time, but even when he admits who he is, Joseph's brothers don't seem to know what to do.

I have wondered about the series of situations that Joseph puts his brothers through before he reveals himself. Was he debating punishing them or was he testing them? It could possibly be both, but I suspect that he was really trying to see whether they had changed. In the final incident, Judah does the opposite for Benjamin to what he did for Joseph. With Joseph, he was the one that suggested selling him; but now, with Benjamin, Judah will risk his future to save his half-brother. He has turned from an instigator to a defender. Joseph can see the family situation has changed and so takes the risk of revealing who he is.

It's a tough moment for the brothers. They know what they did and they've had a taste of what Joseph can inflict on them! This moment is uncertain for both groups. In admitting that they are related, both parties have to face the past, but they also have the chance to explore the future. Things appear to have gone in a full circle and the family is restored.

Families can be a place of both joy and pain. For some, the risk of recognising their relations is similar to Joseph. There is a painful past and an uncertain future. For others, it may be a more positive affirmation of the love that already exists. Yet in both circumstances it can be a cause of tension when one person has more prestige than the rest. Joseph's brothers have been there and done that when it came to jealousy. This time there is no mention of any struggle on that front, just shock!

But if someone close to us is recognised as successful by others, how do we react? We may feel blinded by jealousy; we may lap up the attention that comes from being close to them; we may abuse our relationship to gain influence or possessions; or we may hide from the connection. All these choices can damage our relationship because we no longer see our friend or family member as they are but only through the glare of other people's perceptions.

We may also feel that we are not seen through the reflected light that comes from them. For those who live with leaders there is the challenge of the expectations that come from other people. I grew up the child of Christian leaders and have since become a missionary kid and a pastor's kid. The problem with labels is that they do not only describe but often prescribe. At school people would say, 'You're only a Christian cos your dad's a vicar.' Little did they realise the challenge of maintaining faith when it was so uncool!

By labelling those near leaders and expecting them to live up to certain expectations, we may make it much more difficult for them to be all that God has created them to be. There have been periods in my life where I have felt that I have had to 'face the surname', to do what people expect in order to prove to myself that I won't be put off certain activities because of my name.

But leaders' kids are not all the same. Many lose their faith. For some it is a reaction against the pressure. For others there is the real challenge of whose faith it is – theirs or their parents'. There are questions about how we as members in the church make it easier or more difficult for leaders' kids to find God for themselves. If we mirror the world in our response to those related to leaders, we may only make it more difficult.

If we don't put aside our stereotypes, then we may not hear the way Jesus questioned our perceptions by saying that many of those who are 'first will be last'. If this is true, why is it that we seem to have created a church that functions with the same principles as the rest of society? In saying that those who want to be first need to be the servant of all, Jesus was not only challenging the behaviour of leaders but the attitude of all of us. Are we not called to be different and to function with different principles?

Those in positions of leadership face the challenges that their position entails, but they are not a special breed of human. They make mistakes and are as human as the rest of us. The problem is that if we make them into celebrities then we cease to see them and only view our image of them. Is that not the ultimate illusion of grandeur?

The problem with putting people on pedestals is that we can place expectations on them and their families that are unrealistic and potentially damaging. The challenge for them is not to believe their own publicity and to seek to keep growing in faith regardless. This issue is not exclusive to Christian leaders; it faces all who find themselves in a position of responsibility where others are looking up to them.

Those in leadership have a challenging task. They need our prayers and support, but they do not need our idolatry! If we buy into the power and fame, then we may find that we damage more than we intended. We are part of a family both by birth and also by faith. We need to recognise that we are all significant in the family of God. Each of us can hear from God. Each of us is responsible to use our gifts for the benefit of others. Each of us has something to offer. If we exalt some over the rest of us then we undermine not only the gifts that we each have, but also the giver, God himself.

13 Who are we becoming?

(*Genesis* 45:4–28)

'I am Joseph, your brother whom you sold into Egypt. But don't be angry with yourselves that you did this to me, for God did it. He sent me here ahead of you to preserve your lives … so that you will become a great nation' (*Genesis* 45:4,5,7).

JOSEPH BEGAN AS an apparently ambitious and arrogant young man. He dreamed of glory, with his own family bowing down to him, and now it has happened. The journey of life was not at all as he could have predicted, but now at this climatic moment we discover that Joseph has seen a purpose through it all. The purpose was not located in him and his ability but was revealed in a family and a nation. Ultimately it was about the purposes of God.

Mike had landed on his feet. He left Bristol University with a good degree and got a job in the customer service department of a large firm. In the company, employees were put in teams of 12 and then ranked according to their performance. Mike was doing well – always ranking first or second in his team. In many ways he was the successful one. He had the flat, job and friends. He spent more and more time out with friends from work drinking and having fun. He was a Christian but knew he wasn't living as one. He grew more distant from God. He didn't get into a good church and reading the Bible was slipping down his priority list to once a month. He would become more desperate in his prayers for forgiveness but nothing changed. Eventually his sister said, 'Mike, you've got to get yourself into a good church.'

Mike knew his ambitions and the direction of his life were based on a lie, but convinced himself that it was only for a short time and it didn't really matter. Finally, he decided to move back to Bristol and return to the church he was in during university. He also decided that to get a proper perspective on life, he needed to see how the poor live and what faith looks like when there's little else to hold on to. Going to Uganda for six weeks was a major turning point.

In seeing how others live, Mike discovered a new perspective:

> Somehow I believe we all need to understand God's economy. We are bombarded by messages of what the world values and take on what the world offers. I wear clothes that give identity, not just clothe me … We need to take on what God values. God's economy is utterly upside-down. There are a range of gifts from God. Faith is at the top, money doesn't feature.

After this, Mike resigned from his company and hoped to go into disaster relief work, but through a series of circumstances has found himself with another firm in the same industry. However, this time he seeks to live by different values. When he left university, his priority was to get a good job and his faith suffered. When I asked him recently what he would say to anyone else, he said, 'Find a good church … we are unable to sustain faith without others.'[31]

Mike learned the hard way what it means to set priorities. Some make conscious choices to turn their back on their faith and live differently. But for many others, the journey is much more subconscious with a series of choices that lead us to a very different place to the one we had intended to find ourselves in. Mike initially put a good job at the top of his priority list; he got the job but lost more than he anticipated.

Whether we intend to or not, what we spend our time and energy on reflects what we value most. And it is what we value that we will seek to be successful in. When I asked a friend his opinion on the meaning of success, he responded in the light of a dictionary definition that success is about achieving a desired result:

> Success, thus, has to be considered in light of the desired result. Although, if my desired result is a bonus and I work myself into the ground achieving all kinds of wonderful results in the process but not achieving a bonus, have I been unsuccessful? Or has my success been achieved outside the result I was working for? In other words, the successes achieved that cumulatively might have been considered to be a failure, stand on their own merits as successes. But what if the desired result is wrong/immoral? What then of success?[32]

The question of what we value is important. If our priorities are wrong or immoral then we may achieve the results we aimed for but we may have wasted our time chasing after something that ultimately has little value or is not what we should have invested our life in. It is often said that no one wishes they had spent more time in the office on their death bed. It is easy to get caught up in priorities that at the end of our life suddenly seem much less important. We don't have to stay with our current priorities; maybe it's time to evaluate them!

Joseph's priorities are clear. He sees that God has a bigger purpose in mind so he chooses not to seek vengeance. In this moment, Joseph demonstrated real character. In his humanity, he could have used his power to give his brothers a taste of what they had put him through. Yet he acted not according to a sense of human justice or in response to his personal pain, but rather showed deep compassion. He reached out to his brothers with what they did not deserve – with forgiveness. His graciousness was a reflection of all that God had been doing in his heart and life, but it also pointed to a higher agenda. Joseph had caught a glimpse of why God had allowed all this to happen – so that his people would survive.

Joseph's actions are not to be taken glibly. He had been threatened with death, his own siblings had sold him into slavery with no care for what would happen to him, and then he had endured years in prison. How tempting it would have been to use his power to make them pay! The forgiveness that Joseph extended cost him. It was not something to be taken for granted.

Forgiveness is a tough subject, and one that whole books are written about. For Joseph, the issue was not whether an injustice had taken place but what he would do next. The challenge for Joseph was that the pain had come through those who were supposed to be closest to him. We may relate to this, having been hurt deeply through the actions of family members, friends, spouses, children, or by people in the church. For many people, there are situations in which we know an injustice has taken place, but have yet to make clear our response.

The journey of facing the pain and working through these experiences takes time. These issues are not necessarily easy, but as human beings and as the body of Christ we need each other. Like Joseph, we need to get to a place where we can forgive otherwise we will constantly be riddled with bitterness and anger that will stop us from growing in faith.

Joseph saw the situation in the light of what God was doing through these circumstances. Is it possible for us to get a bigger perspective on the situation? Part of the challenge is not nurturing the hurt by dwelling on the situation in our mind but offering it instead to God. Another aspect is making a conscious effort to reassure the other party. Joseph does not ignore the past but he does not dwell on it either. He quickly emphasises what he understood God was doing through the situation, rather than his brothers' wrongdoing. The fact that Joseph would need to reaffirm this act of forgiveness later in the story suggests that forgiveness has an ongoing element as well.

In what has become known as the Lord's Prayer we say, 'Forgive us our sins as we forgive those that sin against us.' It is in recognising how much we have been forgiven that we forgive. This is not about one-offs: when Peter asked Jesus if he should forgive his brother seven times, Jesus said, 'No! ... seventy times seven' (Matthew 18:22). We are called to forgive, to choose not to recall all that the other person has done, and to seek God's help in order to treat those who have hurt us with the compassion and love that they don't deserve.

As Christians, if we can learn to live as followers of Jesus by hearing the challenge in his words and seek to live as he commanded then this would demonstrate something deep to our friends, family and neighbours. Forgiveness is not about ignoring the pain but facing it. There is no easy formula, but if we don't forgive we are the ones who suffer. We may also make those around us suffer with us. The only way to end the potentially destructive cycle is to seek to obey God and forgive.

In all this, Joseph stands out as someone with deep character and understanding. The positive fruit of all the years of pain seem evident in the way he responds to his brothers. He has the external markers of success (position, wealth, family life, marriage) but has also gained something of greater significance – a depth of character that enables him to both forgive and to reconcile. In our thinking about success, we need to recognise the great value of who we are becoming in terms not only of how we appear but of who we are.

Josephine is a wife and mother of three beautiful girls. She lives in Kenya where she was a teacher. When her girls started school, she could have gone back to work to earn some money but she didn't. She was increasingly aware of the number of people around her who were HIV positive and she wanted to respond.

When I first met her she was volunteering with an organisation to get experience. Once she had completed this, she started meeting with a group of pastors in a poorer community in Nairobi. They were concerned about the spread of HIV in that area and wanted to do something but weren't sure what. So Josephine took four buses a day, crossing the city to get to this community. The work began slowly with much of it done on a voluntary basis.

Initially the pastors were trained to counsel people living with HIV/AIDS. Then members of the congregation were trained in how to provide care for those ill with AIDS-related diseases. These individuals now help their neighbours and refer the more serious cases to two nurses who are involved with the programme. People have found faith through the ministry of Josephine and her team but they have also found compassionate care.

When I asked Josephine about success, I expected her to say it was about caring for others, but she didn't. She said, 'A Christian's success can easily be seen by the fruits of the Holy Spirit that they are bearing.'[33] The fruits that Josephine refers

to are 'love, joy, peace, patience, kindness, goodness, faithfulness, gentleness and self-control' (Galatians 5:22,23).

As I have watched her squat down to hear the whispers of a
sick child or been welcomed into the home of a poor family
who have found support and help through her ministry, I have
been reminded of her words. We are to grow in fruit. Her life is
an example of what this looks like. Fruit may not come cheaply
but it has value.

Therefore success can be understood in terms of the way we
live and the character that we embody. Character is not just
about our attitudes but also about our behaviour. It is reflected in our priorities and our willingness to forgive. But is it
more complex than this?

14 Multi-dimensional living

(*Genesis 46 and 47*)

'I am God,' the voice said, 'the God of your father. Do not be afraid to go down to Egypt, for I will see to it that you become a great nation there. I will go with you down to Egypt, and I will bring your descendants back again.' (*Genesis 46:3,4*).

THE TIME HAS COME for Jacob to meet Joseph again. So Jacob takes his entire family on the journey to Egypt. He's obviously not quite sure about the whole thing because God meets him in a vision to tell him not to be afraid. In God's promise is the reality that Jacob will never see the land again but that God will bring his descendants back to the land that he has promised them.

It was a cold wintry day in Baltimore (near Washington DC). I was at my parents' home and had a big decision to make. I had spent the past year working for the HIV/AIDS department of a large relief and development agency in Kenya. I had the possibility of going back for another year but I just wasn't sure.

A few months earlier, I had been at my Kenyan church's youth group. I went to a small church in the rougher part of town. On my way home, I walked passed the market area, which was bustling with people. It always made me feel nervous walking there because I was such a focus of male attention. It was unusual for a white woman to walk through that area so I would get lots of comments. But that had passed without incident. Now I was moments from home and was thinking about what I would do for the rest of the afternoon. It was drizzling but I felt happy and safe.

Suddenly I felt two hands cover my eyes. I was pulled backwards and found myself sitting in the mud and held down by two strong arms. As one lad held me down, the other guy leaned menacingly over me. I didn't know what they were going to do, nor did I want to find out. Until that moment I didn't know I could scream!

I yelled, kicked and struggled but to no avail. I was pinned to the ground and no one seemed to hear my cries. The high gates on that street remained shut. I couldn't figure out why no one came. My brain went into overdrive and everything went into slow motion. I managed a quick prayer but couldn't see my way out. I had no idea why it was happening. No one tried to grab my purse which made me suspect the worst. Would they rape me? What could I do?

Then something strange happened. The guy holding me down got jittery and left. But the other guy continued to glare menacingly. I was no longer held down but was rooted to the spot by fear. Finally he broke the silence by punching me on the head. Still I couldn't move, even when he appeared to walk away. But he came back with another punch. On the third thump, I jumped into action and ran as fast as my wobbly legs could take me. As I turned, I saw him standing and still staring threateningly at me.

It had all happened months ago. Now I was thousands of miles away in Baltimore, yet the memories still haunted me. I was with my family and felt safe. Did I really want to return to a place shrouded in fear? I prayed and thought. Finally I decided to take the plunge – if God would go with me, then I would go back.

Even though I had made a decision, I still had to face my fears. For a while, every time someone ran from behind me or a man appeared to follow me, I felt petrified that I would be attacked again. A belief that God was with me did not stop me from having emotions but it gave me a deep sense of certainty and the courage to continue. The next year, although challenging, had many moments of joys. I made some deep friendships, had the privilege of working in Rwanda, and learned a lot about trusting God. I look back at that year as very significant, and am grateful that God gave me the strength to return.

Jacob also feared his journey – for why else would God need to comfort him? His grandfather, Abram/Abraham, had been in Egypt. Jacob must have had so many questions. He may have seen the journey to Egypt as a step backwards. His family had land but because of the famine, they were fleeing to Egypt as refugees. In Jacob's reflections, there may have been a sense of failure as well as fear. He would be going to a strange land because he was not able to save his family on his own land. Now he would be relying on his son rather than saving the family himself.

It is not possible to state exactly what Jacob was feeling, yet the Bible reveals how God spoken into this mix of emotions to reassure Jacob of his presence and his purpose. This moment that may have felt like a disaster to Jacob was actually a necessary step in all that God was going to do. The exodus and God's rescuing of his people from Egypt could only happen if Jacob took the family to Egypt in the first place.

God gives Jacob a hint of this. He assures Jacob that he will fulfil the promise to Abraham and create a great nation from their descendants. He also affirms that this step is necessary in that process. Jacob may not be able to see what will happen, but God assures him that there is a bigger picture. God tells Jacob what we can see in the light of history – this moment is necessary and significant, even if the immediate context feels far from positive.

In this way, Jacob has a glimpse of what it means to live multi-dimensionally. Naturally he would only see this move within the context of his immediate situation. His thoughts and emotions would be focused on his present dimension. Yet God speaks to him of another dimension – the future. This moment that in the present may have felt like a failure, would gain significance in the light of the future. It would also give him a sense of hope amidst his fear.

This challenge to Jacob also questions the way we view things. Even in our own lifetime, what we think is successful may change. As children, we may have thought we would be a footballer, nurse, teacher, millionaire etc. As we grow older our priorities can change and we may end up in a very different role than we had initially intended. In this process, even our concept of success and failure may change as our goals shift and as we meet different people and hear their approaches to life and success. Yet within all this, our focus tends to remain in our current context. We evaluate our life within the framework of our family, friends and broader social context. We tend to live in one dimension – the here and now!

God's words to Jacob remind us that there is a different dimension altogether. There is the eternal dimension. We can get so consumed by our present context that we lose sight of the big picture of what God is doing. We are warned in the Bible to watch and pray for Christ's return. It is clear that we don't know when this will happen but that we need to be ready. The danger is that we don't view our lives in the big picture and so are consumed by petty things rather than seeking to know God and to share him with others so that together we are more prepared to spend eternity with him.

Having said this, our current struggles may make little sense to us. Given a larger perspective and in the light of history, they may take on value and meaning but at the time it may just feel confusing and frustrating. And there are moments that seem to make no sense at all. There are times that God may choose to speak into our situation to bring comfort and assure us that he is still at work. Yet there are times that silence seems to be all that we hear. In both situations, the challenge for us is the same as the challenge for Jacob – to trust that God is there and has a purpose, even when we can't see it.

I have a friend who often says, 'I don't know what God is doing but I am sure he is doing something!' We may feel that we have to have all the answers, especially with friends who do not share our faith, but we don't. We are *not* God; we do not see the past, the present and the future, so there is some mystery in life. Trust is not a form of fatalism – whatever will be will be – it is an active choice. We choose to trust that God sees the big picture when we clearly don't. We recognise that his perspective is different from ours. We choose to keep following even when it gets to the point of, 'I do believe; help me overcome my unbelief!' (Mark 9:24, NIV).

The Bible describes faith as 'being sure of what we hope for and certain of what we do not see' (Hebrews 11:1, NIV). There are moments when this certainty dims and we may feel like a failure as a Christian. Yet it is at these moments, as we cling desperately to what we know of God, that God often takes us deeper in our walk with him. It is in such moments that multi-dimensional living is essential.

Months after being attacked, I really questioned how God could let it happen. I thought I was in the place where God wanted me to be, so surely it shouldn't have happened? I felt like a failure. For all my attempts at being streetwise, I had not been able to stop it from happening and for some reason, neither had God. I didn't believe that God had caused it but I do think he allowed it. Why?

After a while, I choose not to think about it. I felt like it would only drive me mad to dwell on it. It wasn't until two years of living in the UK, that I started to feel safe again. I know that it could have happened anywhere but I am still not sure why it did. Yet through all the questions and confusion, I have learned more about trusting God when life doesn't make rational sense!

In this way, a moment that may be a failure in the eyes of others and even ourselves can actually be a moment of real significance as our faith deepens. This may then suggest that our very concept of success is ultimately flawed, if what we value does not have significance in the light of eternity. The challenge, then, is to discover what really counts. Presumably the only way to do this is to allow the one who knows eternity to challenge the way we perceive our lives and our assumptions about what is important.

It is in this context that many of Jesus' words stand as both a rebuke and a challenge. In one of the parables he told about the kingdom of heaven, an owner of an estate goes out to get workers and agrees a wage with them. As the day goes on, he hires more people. Eventually, at the end of the day he pays those he hired last the same wage as those he hired first. The people who were hired first complain about this but the owner affirms his right to be generous. The final words in the story are, 'And so it is, that many who are first now will be last then; and those who are last now will be first then' (Matthew 20:16).

If we had been one of those hired at the beginning of the day, we may also have complained. It seems unjust that those who worked the shortest amount of time should benefit equally. We all have our ideas about what seems fair and right, yet Jesus turns everything upside down. If we could see our life in the context of eternity, would we get an uncomfortable shock? Would we find ourselves at the back when we think we should be at the front? What can we do about it?

Jesus answers the question with a command:

> Do not store up for yourselves treasures on earth, where moth and rust destroy, and where thieves break in and steal. But store up for yourselves treasures in heaven, where moth and rust do not destroy, and where thieves do not break in and steal. For where your treasure is, there your heart will be also. (*Matthew* 6:19–21, NIV)

If we are to invest our lives in eternal treasure then we need to explore what this means. The word 'treasure' in the original Greek is the same both times it is used. This does not illuminate what is meant by this treasure that lasts and the treasure which does not. Therefore the context of the passage needs to be looked at. This passage comes in what is known as the 'Sermon on the Mount', a series of teaching about how we live. It fits between teaching on loving your enemies and not worrying about the future, between giving to the needy and not being able to serve both God and money. The context suggests that the treasure which really counts is not about physical items but is reflected in our attitudes towards others and our trust in God.

A friend of mine became a Christian in her early twenties. We were walking in the Yorkshire Dales and talking about the challenges of faith. She had been a follower of Jesus for two years but was struggling with a number of questions. Then she turned to me and said, 'I feel like I've gone too far to ask the basic questions!' I suspect that's part of the challenge. Even in faith, we like to think that we have made it but we can not afford to get comfortable because when we stop moving forwards, we start going backwards. There is always more to learn about who God is. It is not too late to ask where our priorities lie and what kind of treasure we are saving.

In reading the Bible, in talking to friends, in asking questions, in prayer and silence, in multiple ways we need to keep seeking after God. Yet we also need to recognise that God has reached out to us and we need to learn what it is to rest in his presence. As God challenges our assumptions and shapes our heart and attitudes then we will grow in our ability to understand what is really important. The challenge is not to be so absorbed by this life that we lose sight of eternity. In this way our apparent successes and failures may take on a very different meaning.

15 Transformed for action

(*Genesis* 49:29 – 50:26)

But Joseph told them, 'Don't be afraid of me. Am I
God to judge and punish you? As far as I am concerned, God turned into good what you meant for
evil. He brought me to the high position I have
today so I could save the lives of many people'
(*Genesis* 50:19,20).

AT THEIR FATHER'S death, Joseph's brothers panic: will their
brother now get his revenge because their father is no longer
around to protect them? In a cold sweat they concoct a story to
say that on his death bed their father insisted on Joseph's
continued protection of them. Yet they have completely
missed the point. Joseph has no desire to get his revenge; he
will continue to hold that God had a higher purpose in it all.
He has been changed and his father's death won't reverse the
process.

It was a hot June day, so we relished the coolness of the
garden. This was a dream of my dad's. He loves Israel and had
always wanted to bring us, his family, to see it. We had spent
the day visiting the sites in Jerusalem. We'd walked through
crowded streets of bustling shoppers, joined the throngs

visiting the Wailing Wall and wandered in the Garden of Gethsemane.

Eventually we arrived in another garden not far from the Damascus Gate. We turned right and walked along the path towards a raised platform area. As we drew closer the peace of the garden was shattered. The platform looked out on the busy bus station. Above the jostling figures and moving vehicles is a cliff face that looks like a skull. Was this the 'skull hill' mentioned in the Bible? Could this noisy bus station in fact be the place where Jesus died?

If so, there would need to be a tomb nearby to save the danger of carrying Jesus' dead body through the streets of Jerusalem. As we walked through the garden we saw a well and a wine press, signs that the owner must have been a wealthy person. This fits with the description of Joseph of Arimathea in the Bible who asked if he could bury Jesus' body (Luke 23:50–53).

Finally we turned a corner and in front of us down some steps was a tomb carved in the rock. Outside the tomb is a groove where the stone would have been rolled and the remains of a baptistery with a first century anchor carved in the wall. Then we entered the tomb. It was not dark and scary, but cool and relatively light.

We walked into the room and then turned right to look at where the bodies would have been laid. I had always assumed that the bodies would have been laid on raised benches, but the resting places were sunk in the rock. There were two resting places; one was incomplete and was presumably intended for the owner's wife who was never laid in it because it was never finished. The other was complete but appeared to have been hurriedly lengthened. A strange thing to do when tombs were built for a particular person while they were still alive! Therefore, the resting place seems to have been used by someone other than the one it was originally intended for.

Here in the Garden Tomb, the place where it is argued that Jesus was buried and rose again, I felt a sense of God's presence. What hit me most in this eerie yet strangely evocative place were the words that ring down the centuries: 'Why do you look for the living among the dead? He is not here; he has risen' (Luke 24:5,6, NIV).

However, in reflecting on one death, we are reminded of another. In Jesus' family tree, we discover that he is related back to Jacob (Matthew 1:2). Now Jacob has died and Joseph's brothers start to panic. They are worried about what Joseph will do now that the restraining hand of their father has gone. They think that Joseph's kindness was only an act and now he will take his revenge. Joseph has wept over them, forgiven them, and provided for them; yet they still can't see it as genuine. The possibility that something has happened deep within Joseph to change him radically was beyond their comprehension.

Yet Joseph is different. He now sees the events of his life within a bigger picture. He has realised that life is not all about him and what happens to him. He has caught a glimpse of what it means for God to take a situation and to change it; to take individuals and transform them; to take a people and to save them.

To think of success simply as doing what you set out to seems inadequate in the light of this final scene in Joseph's life. I doubt Joseph initially intended to be so gracious to his brothers. However, his words at the end made him sound like he has a much better grasp of what's really important than his brothers do. He sounds like he knows what really matters – to see beyond the immediate to what God is doing through a situation, and what his role in this should be so that others may be helped.

Through his life, Joseph was transformed. He could have spent his life bitter and angry, or he could have been consumed by the hopelessness of his circumstances and sought to end his life. But in fact he did not allow his circumstances to crush his spirit or embitter his heart. He continued to work hard and act responsibly whether as a slave, prisoner or Prime Minister. He did not allow his role to determine his commitment to act with integrity as in the situation with Potiphar's wife. Some of this may well be a reflection of his character, maturity and determination, but one is entitled to suspect that it is also because he allowed God to transform him.

It is easy to place an emphasis on appearing successful in our cultural context, rather than living significantly. We may become so earth-focused that we are blind to the big picture. We can invest heavily in possessions, shares, relationships and work – potentially good things but with a limited shelf-life. We grasp at our illusions of grandeur rather than emphasising that which has eternal value. In effect we 'confuse heaven's radiant stars with a duck's footprint left in the mud'.[34]

Why do we do this when we can read in the Bible what is important to God? God clearly states his love for human beings and desire for them to know him. But knowing God can never be an end in itself. As the writer of James says, 'Faith that doesn't show itself by good deeds is no faith at all – it is dead and useless' (James 2:17). Our faith is to transform us for action. It is not enough simply to believe in God; we have to live for him and so share his love with others. Otherwise our lives may suggest that we follow a dead Lord rather than a risen Christ.

The challenge of the tomb is the challenge for us all: 'Don't be afraid! Go tell...' (Matthew 28:10). There is a risk in leading a life that seeks to live out what we believe. We don't know what God will call us to. Sometimes the hardest challenge is to live for him where he's placed us.

Fear can stop us from being all that we can be. Fear of failure, fear of the unknown, fear of many things can paralyse us. It can stop us from sharing our faith with others, of reaching out with compassion to the poor or challenging injustice. It stopped Joseph's brothers from trusting his intentions and it can stop us from living a full life in the sight of the God we trust. Ultimately it is fear that will rob us of the joy that comes from seeking to follow Jesus in loving obedience.

The issue then is not what we earn, how we look, or what people call us, but where we are heading. Do we know God for ourselves and are we ready to share him with others? Reading a book like this may be an interesting pastime but it is not enough. The difficulty with such a redefinition is that our normal ways of measuring achievement no longer apply. It has less to do with quantity and more to do with quality. It cannot be measured by dress size, our total earnings, and the number of gadgets we own, nor necessarily by the amount of time spent reading our Bible, the money given to charity or the number of church services we go to.

Instead of seeking to weigh our achievements, we are called to look in the mirror. In exploring the questions of success, we need to be prepared to re-examine our own lives in the light of our faith. The word 'Christian' means a follower of Jesus. The real issue is the degree to which we are following. In John's Gospel, Jesus outlines what this means in a conversation with his disciples, just before his death and resurrection. He says, 'If you love me, obey my commandments' (John 14:15). It is not enough for us to claim to follow Jesus and not to do what he says. Obedience is not a popular concept in our individualised world and can be seen as a very passive term. Yet obedience is really an active choice – will I do what has been said or do what I want to instead? It is not simply a decision made once but a constant choice to keep obeying what Jesus said in the Bible. We may talk a lot about loving God and seeking to follow Jesus, but the real question is, how much are we obeying his commands?

Yet the passage goes on:

> If you love me, obey my commandments. And I will ask the Father, and he will give you another Counsellor, who will never leave you. He is the Holy Spirit, who leads into all truth. The world at large cannot receive him, because it isn't looking for him and doesn't recognise him. But you do, because he lives with you now and later will be in you. (John 14:15–17)

It is tempting to think that we can somehow transform ourselves into obedient followers. That doesn't seem to be what Jesus was getting at. It is not through our sheer will, determination and hard work that we will obey. God is not a big teacher figure with a stick. If obedience is linked to love then it would appear that the more we know God, the more we will want to do as he says. But even this may be very much our own choice and effort. Jesus clearly states that God the Father continues to be involved in the process by sending the Holy Spirit.

For the disciples, the Holy Spirit would not dwell in them until after the resurrection. For us, God the Father sends the Holy Spirit to dwell in us when we believe so that we will grow in our understanding and knowledge of him. There is a combination of God drawing us to him and us choosing to follow. It is out of this relationship that we will naturally want to share what we are discovering of God with others. As we grow, God will be changing us and so our action flows from a deeper knowledge of him and is more likely to have eternal value.

We started this chapter in a garden, and will end it in another garden. On my last day in Israel, I went to the Garden of Gethsemane. As I sat on a rock looking out across the valley to the city of Jerusalem, I was reminded of another incident in the same place.

Jesus came to Gethsemane on the night he was betrayed. He knew what was coming. It was no light matter. He felt the emotional agony of this moment so he came to pray. In his grief, he asked his Father to remove from him that which was to follow. Yet as he wrestled with the future, he made a choice. He chose obedience: 'Yet I want your will not mine' (Matthew 26:39).

In this moment there is both comfort and a question. There is comfort in knowing that as Jesus wrestled with what he knew his Father wanted, so we are not alone in struggling with what we know God is calling us to do. We should not look down on ourselves because we find it difficult to live life for the glory of God. It is normal to find this challenging at times. Yet a question remains: will we follow God's will or our own?

There may be times of wrestling as we explore the question of success and the areas where we have illusions of grandeur. It is likely to be painful at times as we re-evaluate what we value and allow God to challenge our priorities. But if we hide from the struggle, we only affirm that our illusions are more important to us than knowing God.

Ultimately success in kingdom terms is about loving God in obedience and trust and loving each other out of the love that is in God's very nature. Are we ready to continue being transformed for action? Are we willing to take a risk and seek to live out our faith where we are? There is a choice: illusions of grandeur or eternal treasure. How will we invest?

References

Articles

D Barr, 'Crying on the Inside' in *The Times*, (1 May 2004).

S Kaufman, www.bbc.co.uk/blast/art/profiles/artprofile_skaufman.shtml (Internet, 2003).

Books

Oswald Chambers, *My Utmost for His Highest*, (Discovery House Publishers, 1992).

VE Frankl, *Man's Search for Meaning*, (Washington Square Press Publication, 1985).

VP Hamilton, *The Book of Genesis, Chapters 18-50*, (Eerdmans, 1995).

Victor Hugo, *Les Misérables*, (Penguin Putnam, 1987).

Donald Kraybill, *The Upside-Down Kingdom*, (Herald Press, 1978).

Watchman Nee, *What Shall This Man Do?*, (Victory Press, 1973).

JRR Tolkien, *The Lord of the Rings: Fellowship of the Rings*, (Harper Collins, 1993).

Brother Yun with Paul Hattaway, *The Heavenly Man*, (Monarch, 2002).

Films

A Knight's Tale, (Columbia Pictures, 2001).

Notting Hill, (Universal Studios, 2002).

Pay it Forward, (Warner Bros., 2000).

Phone Booth, (Fox, 2003).

Robin Hood, Prince of Thieves, (Morgan Creek Productions, Inc., and Warner Bros. Inc., 1991).

Shark Tale, (Dreamworks, 2005).

Small-group material

THIS MATERIAL IS designed to help small groups work through particular issues outlined in each chapter of this book. This material is designed to be flexible, as people are different and groups function in various ways. Therefore more creative or more discursive introductions are outlined, wherever possible. Then there is a section entitled 'Exploration' which seeks to look more deeply at the story of Joseph for that chapter. This is followed by 'Reflection', which aims to help the group think about the issue in the light of their own situation either corporately or individually. The hope is that this material will be used in the most appropriate way for each group so that together we may discover more of the lessons that can be learned from the story of Joseph.

1: Yearning for more

Aim: To consider what we mean by success and to start to ask the question about whether our perspective needs to be revised.

Introduction:

Success is…?

This question can be considered in several ways:

- Ask the group to define success.

- There is a series of cartoons beginning with 'Love is…' These were recently used as posters on the British tube to address different behaviours and to encourage commuters to show more courtesy; eg 'Love is… letting others off first.' Ask members of the group, either in groups or individually, to come up with a strapline for success. These can be humorous or serious. So 'Success is…'

- Ask each member to choose an image from a magazine or newspaper that they think defines success and to share this with the group.

Exploration:

Read Genesis 49:22–26. The following are possible questions that can be used to explore the meaning of the text further:

Read Genesis 49:1 – what is the context of this passage?

What images are used to describe who Joseph is?

What do we learn about Joseph's story from this blessing?

What would it look like for us to be a prince or princess among our family or friends?

Are there elements of this blessing that we relate to and why?

If we compare our definition of success and this passage, how would we re-define our original ideas?

Reflection:

Consider individually or as a group, the quote from Stu Shepherd.

Have we 'died to the things we value most'?

As we talk about success, are there areas where our attitudes need to change?

Are we willing to be vulnerable with God and each other as we explore this further?

Pray for each other that God might teach us more of what is really important in life through the next few weeks.

2: Glory seekers (Genesis 37:1–11)

Aim: To explore the issue of ambition and what it means to follow God wholeheartedly.

Introduction:

Imagine you have reached the 'top of the reef' – what does it look like?

This can be done in several ways. For example:

- As a discussion – the group could be given a few minutes to consider the question before discussing it further.

- Through pictures – each member of the group could be asked to draw their response and then explain their picture.

- Through images – the group could be given magazines, paper and glue so that they can create a collage to illustrate their response and then describe it.

Exploration:

Read Genesis 37:1–11:

How did Joseph describe the 'top of the reef'?

How did his family respond to his comments?

What similarities are there between our image of the 'top of the reef' and Joseph's?

What can we learn from this story about motivation and handling ambition?

Reflection:

Time of quiet reflection. It may be helpful to ask the group to write their responses down so that they can reflect on them later.

What would it mean for us to 'Do whatever he tells you' (John 2:5)?

Should our image of 'top of the reef' change?

3: Vying for attention (Genesis 37:12–35)

Aim: To consider the challenge of rivalry and ways to stop the situation from escalating.

Introduction:

What is rivalry?

This can be done in several ways. For example:

- By sharing ideas – members of the group could be encouraged to share their ideas on this and any examples that they know of.

- Through a film clip (eg *Romeo and Juliet*) – the group could watch a clip and then discuss what rivalry looked like in the film and the types of rivalry that exist today.

- Through stories – the group could be asked to look through some newspapers and pull out stories that illustrate rivalry to help the group discuss it.

Exploration: Read Genesis 37:12–35:

How do the events of this story unfold?

What would it feel like to be one of Joseph's brothers?

What can we learn from the reaction of Joseph's brothers about the effect of rivalry?

What could have been done to stop the situation from escalating?

Reflection:

The challenge with jealousy and rivalry is that it can have a domino effect with such destructive results. [This could be illustrated by lining up a number of dominos and describing the situation in the film, one of the stories or in Joseph's life and then knocking them all down.]

Where have you experienced rivalry and jealousy?

What was it like to be in this situation?

Was it worked through?

What can we do to stop jealousy and rivalry from taking hold of relationships?

What can we learn from the example of Peter about how to respond when it all goes wrong?

4: Valuing the ordinary (Genesis 37:36; 39:1–5)

Aim: To consider ways of living our lives extraordinarily by valuing each day and recognising that God is with us.

Introduction:

Read the opening story in the text.

- Ask members of the group to reflect quietly on situations where their response now will impact who they become.

- Ask the group to discuss whether they think there is a link between our responses and how we grow as people. This could also be considered in the light of Romans 5:3–5.

- Ask people to share stories of how a change in response has led to a different conclusion than would otherwise have been expected.

Exploration:

Read Genesis 37:36; 39:1–5.

How does Joseph's current situation contrast to his earlier life?

How did Joseph respond to his new situation?

What can we learn from Joseph about what it means to live in challenging situations?

Reflection:

Consider the Oswald Chambers' quote (p47).

Where do we find it challenging to 'be exceptional in the ordinary things of life'?

It may be helpful to have a time of prayer for each other that we may have the courage to live exceptionally in the places God has put us.

5: Choosing to be different (Genesis 39:6–20)

Aim: To reflect on the principles that govern our lives and on how to choose to be different.

Introduction:

What principles govern our lives? How do we decide what's important?

The following three suggestions would provide different angles for exploring this topic.

- *'You are walking down the street and suddenly you are caught up in a whirlwind and deposited on a strange island. People live there. They wear different clothes, eat unusual food and follow different customs. You are very much the stranger. They are fascinated by you and ask you to describe the life you used to lead. As you talk you start to hear the priorities behind your words. You suddenly wake up and realise it is all a dream but you realise that you have a choice: will you live by your old priorities? If not, how will you decide what's important?'*

  The hope is that as the group discuss this, it will become clear what principles govern their lives, how they use their time, money, possessions etc, and so what is important to them and what they would like to change.

- A clip from a film like *Castaway* could be used to help the group either reflect what the priorities are for those in the film or what theirs would be if they were in the same position. If they or the characters in the film were suddenly returned home, what principles for living would they want to ensure they maintained?

- Members of the group could be asked to write down a timetable for their typical day. They would then be asked to reflect on what this says about their priorities. As a group, people could share different priorities that they thought were reflected. Then the group could discuss what priorities they would like to include and how this could be done.

Exploration:

Read Genesis 39:6–20.

What challenge faced Joseph?

How does Joseph handle the situation that he finds himself in?

How does Potiphar's wife handle the situation?

What insights can we gain from Potiphar's wife's response about how people may try to question our convictions?

What can we learn from Joseph about how to live by our principles?

Reflection:

What does it mean for us to live as Christians where we are?

Are we willing to be distinctive?

6: Faithfulness rewarded (*Genesis* 39:20–23)

Aim: To explore what it means to live as a Christian when life feels limited.

Introduction:

How have we felt boxed in by circumstances?

This is an opportunity for the group to share their stories about when, like Alison, they have felt trapped by invisible bars.

Exploration:

Read Genesis 39:20–23.

What caused this situation?

What do you feel about Potiphar's reaction?

How did Joseph respond to his situation?

If CCTV cameras existed at that time, what do you think we could learn from watching Joseph?

Reflection:

Read the quote from Lord of the Rings (p62).

What situations face us that we wish didn't?

What lessons do we want to take from today into the week ahead?

7: Downwards is upwards (*Genesis* 40:1–22)

Aim: To examine our own situations and ask whether we are willing to allow God to use us or whether we seek to do everything ourselves.

Introduction:

What does it look like for God to use someone?

This could be done by:

- Members of the group sharing stories of how they have felt God use them. How did they know and what did they learn from these situations?

- Discussing two to five stories in the Bible of how God used different people, and asking what it looked like for God to use them and what it might look like for God to use us.

Exploration:

Read Genesis 40:1–22. The following are possible questions that can be used to explore the meaning of the text further:

Who are the different characters in this passage?

Imagine yourself as each of these characters. What do you think they would be feeling?

What did Joseph need to do in order for God to use him?

What can we learn from Joseph's response to the chief baker and chief cup-bearer?

Are there areas where we need to acknowledge that what happens is 'God's business' and not ours, but we are willing for him to use us if he chooses?

Do we think that there are places where God can't use us? If so, what can we learn from the story of Joseph about this?

Reflection:

Imagine this week that you are playing Pay it Forward. *Ask God how he would like to use you to help at least one person.*

If people are willing to share this with the group, then people can pray for each other on the night and during the week and hopefully share what happened next week.

8: Frustrated? (*Genesis* 40:23; 41:1)

Aim: To consider whether God can use frustrating times to help us grow and what this means as we look at our own lives.

Introduction:

Read Trinny's story.

> Is it helpful to think of life as like a jigsaw?

This might best be done creatively, but the following are some suggestions:

- Ask each member to draw on a piece of paper the beginnings of a jigsaw and name the different pieces with different moments in their life. Reflecting on their paper, ask members whether they think this is a helpful way to look at life.

- Start a discussion among the group by asking them what different analogies we can use for life and whether the jigsaw is a helpful one and why.

- Break the group into two or three teams, each with a jigsaw. Tell them it is a competition to see which team can get the furthest with the jigsaw in the set time. Once you have ended the competition, ask the group what it was like to work on the jigsaw. Was it easy? What were the challenges? What issues arose? And then use this discussion to ask whether thinking of our lives as a jigsaw is helpful.

Exploration:

Read Genesis 40:23 and 41:1.

> If Joseph's life is like a jigsaw, what pieces are currently in place?
>
> What word(s) strikes you from this passage? And why?
>
> How do you think Joseph would have felt?
>
> Does this story remind you of any situations that you have been through? What did you learn from these experiences?

148

Reflection:

Are there elements of this story that relate to our current situation or the situations of people that we know?

This would be an opportunity to share these stories and to pray for these situations.

9: Stored strength (Genesis 41:1–36)

Aim: To explore what it means to store up strength in the good times in order to help us in the tough ones; and to look at what it means to implement the dreams/ideas that God has given us.

Introduction:

If our life was a skyscraper or a tree, what would the foundations/roots look like?

This could be looked at in several ways:

- Ask each of the members of the group to draw a tree or skyscraper on a piece of paper and label those things that they think are above ground and those that are the foundations of their life.

- If people are uncomfortable drawing, a similar thing can be done by folding a piece of paper in half and then opening it again. On one side of the crease write all the elements of life that can be seen by others, and on the other side, all those elements that the person would consider to be part of the foundations of their life.

- Talk as a group about Cheryl's story and what has enabled her to keep going in tough times. From this, encourage members of the group to share what experiences they think have been foundational in their life, that give them strength in more challenging times.

Exploration:

Read Genesis 41:1–36.

What issue does Joseph face?

What plan does Joseph propose?

What can we learn from Joseph's response?

What type of strength could we store in the good times? How do we do this?

Reflection:

This could either be a time of prayer for those struggling with different pressures and/or an opportunity to look at implementing our dreams and then praying that we might have the wisdom and courage to do this. Possible questions include:

What dreams/ideas have you felt were from God and never acted on?

What stopped you from doing it?

Are there things that we can still do about this?

10: Fame and faithfulness (*Genesis* 41:37-52)

Aim: To explore how we define ourselves, and what it means to follow God in any situation.

Introduction:

The following are suggestions for considering the issue of fame and the future:

- Discuss whether you agree with what Julia Roberts says to Hugh Grant in *Notting Hill*: 'The fame thing isn't really real, you know.'[35] This could be done either by looking at this quote or after watching the clip from the film. What is fame? Is it worth aiming at? What does it mean for it not to be 'really real'?

- Ask the group to share their hopes and ambitions for the future. In thinking about this, what potential dangers are there in losing sight of what really matters? How can we stay focused? How do we determine what is important?

Exploration:

Read Genesis 41:37–52.

How does Joseph's situation here contrast to the situation described in the earlier chapters of Genesis?

How does Joseph understand his situation?

Imagine that you are Joseph. How do you think he feels at this moment?

Have you had any experience that is similar to this? How did you feel? What did you do?

What can we learn from this?

Reflection:

The following questions are suggestions of how to explore this issue further:

What gifts do we think God has given us?

What do we think about the suggestion that if we undermine our gifts then we also undermine the God who gives them?

How can we value who we are without getting proud?

What does it mean to follow God in every situation?

How can this help us think through our home, work or college situation and the attitudes we want to portray there?

As role models, what would we like to demonstrate to those around us?

This session could be ended with a time of prayer that we might become people whom others recognise as having God's Spirit.

11: Beyond ourselves (*Genesis* 41:53–57)

Aim: To explore what it means to have concern for others.

Introduction:

Read Tina's story.

What situations do we find difficult? What can we learn from Tina's honesty?

Exploration:

Read Genesis 41:53–57.

How do the different people respond to the famine?

How does this relate to the different ways we respond to difficult situations?

What can we learn from Joseph's response?

Reflection:

What are the things that we have?

How can we use them to help others?

It might be helpful to consider as a group how to respond to the needs of others. What are individuals in the group doing to help others? How can the group support them in this? Are there things that could be done corporately?

12: Family matters (*Genesis* 42:1 – 45:3)

Aim: To consider our response to those in leadership and how we affirm each other in the body of Christ.

Introduction:

There are a number of ways that this could be done:

- Discuss: *You receive a letter from the solicitor announcing that a relative has left you enough money to make you a millionaire. How do you think this would change your view of yourself and other people's view of you?*

- Set up a *Monopoly* board as an illustration. Suggest that one person has won lots of properties and the others have very little. Ask people what they would think of that individual and how their feelings would change. Ask the person who is thought to be the wealthy one in the game how they think this would change their attitudes.

Exploration:

Read Genesis 44:1 – 45:3. The following questions are suggestions for exploring the passage further:

How does Joseph use his money and position?

How do Joseph's brothers react to his accusations?

How has Judah changed (compare this with Genesis 37:26,27)?

The brothers' had been jealous of Joseph in the past; how do they respond now when he reveals himself?

Why do you think Joseph's brothers had been blinded to him before?

What can we learn from this story?

Reflection:

How do we respond to those that we know who gain earthly recognition?

What can we do to help those in leadership?

Where do our attitudes need to change?

This could lead to a time of prayer for those in leadership either of the church, the country or individuals that are known to the group.

13: Who are we becoming? (*Genesis 45:4–28*)

Aim: To ask the question, 'Who are we becoming?'

Introduction:

This issue could be considered through:

- Reading and discussing Mike's story. Who did Mike want to become and how has this changed? What can we learn from his experience?

- Writing our epitaph. It sounds morbid, but how would we like to be remembered? What would we like people to say about us on our death? This shows what we want to become.

- Discuss the quote about 'desired results'. Is what we think we want, really what we want? Are there areas of our lives that we need to re-evaluate?

Exploration:

Read Genesis 45:4–28.

> *How does Joseph understand all that has happened to him?*
>
> *What do you think it would feel like to have been one of Joseph's brothers at this moment?*
>
> *What process does Joseph go through in talking to his brothers?*
>
> *Are there situations where we need to forgive?*
>
> *What can we learn from Joseph about how to do this?*

Reflection:

Read Galatians 5:22,23.

> *What areas of fruit would we like to grow in?*

Pray as a group for each other that we might grow in fruit. Encourage each member to continue praying about this during the week and asking God to enable us to grow in this area.

14: Multi-dimensional living *(Genesis 46 and 47)*

Aim: To consider what it means to look at life within the context of our whole life and eternity and not just the immediate situation.

Introduction:

Here are a couple of different ways to start:

- Read the opening story. What can we learn from this? Is it possible to trust God even when nothing makes sense?

- Imagine you are Cinderella at the end of her life. What would you remember and why?

- Ask the group to share their own story of moments when they didn't understand what God was doing but they had to just trust that God knew. What did they learn from this?

Exploration:

Read Genesis 46:1–5.

What changes are occurring to the family of Joseph?

What do you think was going through Jacob's mind?

Why do you think God decided to meet Jacob in a dream?

Where do we find it difficult to trust God?

How does God tend to meet us when we are unsure?

What can we learn from this?

Reflection:

Read Matthew 6:19–21 and talk about what it means to store treasure in heaven.

What does this look like?

What stops us from doing this? What are our fears about this?

How can we change?

Pray for each other, and end with the reminder that 'where your treasure is, there your heart will be also' (Matthew 6:21, NIV).

15: Transformed for action (*Genesis* 49:29 – 50:26)

Aim: To explore what to do with what's been discussed in this book.

Introduction:

> *Imagine you are in the Garden of Gethsemane. What must you face in your own life, that you need God's strength for?*

This would be an opportunity for members of the group to share their struggles and the areas that God is teaching them on.

Exploration:

Read Genesis 50:15–26.

> *Why does Joseph weep?*
>
> *How does Joseph seek to comfort his brothers?*
>
> *Which character do we relate to in this story and why?*
>
> *Are there situations that we find it hard to accept forgiveness?*
>
> *Are we willing for God to change us so that we can reveal him to others?*

Reflection:

Ask the group to write on one side of paper one to three things that they have learned during the weeks. Then on the other side to write one to three things that they have decided to change or do because of what they've learned. To help people remember, this could become a bookmark in their Bible or be put somewhere that they will look at it again. Then the group can share these and decide how they will help each other to do what they have said they would do. The group can also pray for each other in these areas.

Endnotes

1 V Calver, Unpublished poem
2 *Phone Booth*, (Fox, 2003)
3 D. Barr, '*Crying on the Inside*' in The Times, p12
4 *Robin Hood, Prince of Thieves*, (Morgan Creek Productions, Inc., and Warner Bros. Inc., 1991)
5 *Shark Tale*, (Dreamworks, 2005)
6 Conversation, May 2004.
7 *California Dreaming*, (2005)
8 Conversation, 7 July 2002
9 V P Hamilton, *The Book of Genesis*: Chapters 18–50 (1995), p459
10 Oswald Chambers, *My Utmost for His Highest* (1992), Oct 21 reading
11 Email, 24 October 2004
12 V P Hamilton, *The Book of Genesis*: Chapters 18-50, p460
13 Watchman Nee, *What shall this man do?* (1973), p188
14 Conversation, February 2005
15 JRR Tolkien, *The Lord of the Rings:Fellowship of the Ring* (1954), p78
16 Sermon tape, 7 August 2005
17 Conversation, 13 June 2005
18 Donald Kraybill, *The Upside-Down Kingdom* (1978; revised 2003)
19 Notes of a conversation, 26 March 2005
20 Email verification, 20 August 2005
21 Brother Yun, *The Heavenly Man* (2002), pp310,311
22 Conversation, 25 September 2004
23 Personal correspondence, 19 July 2005
24 Questionnaire, 28 July 2004
25 Notes of a conversation, 18 July 2005
26 Personal correspondence, 19 July 2005
27 Conversation, June 2004
28 S Kaufman, www.bbc.co.uk/blast/art/profiles/artprofile_skaufman.shtml
29 V Frankl, *Man's Search for Meaning* (1962), p86
30 V P Hamilton, *The Book of Genesis: Chapters 18-50* (1995), p513
31 Notes of a conversation, 9 March 2005
32 Questionnaire, 28 July 2004
33 Questionnaire, 19 July 2004
34 V Hugo, *Les Misérables* (1862), p52
35 *Notting Hill*, (Universal Studios, 2002)

Other Resources from Scripture Union

90,000 Hours: managing the world of work

Rodney Green   ISBN: 1 85999 594 2   £6.99

Most of us will spend 90,000 hours of our lives at work. How do we view this time? Does God want us to see our work as worthwhile in itself? Examining the themes of creativity, rest, harmony and perseverance from a biblical perspective, Rodney Green argues that this is indeed the case.

B format, 160pp

Thank God it's Monday: ministry in the workplace

Mark Greene   ISBN: 1 85999 208 0   £6.99

Fun, fast, and full of stories, this highly practical book looks at how we can make the most of the time we spend at work. This updated and expanded edition includes a new chapter on the ethical challenges that face us and a revised resource section.

B format, 180pp

The Lost Art of Meditation: deepening your prayer life

Sheila Pritchard   ISBN: 1 85999 643 4   £6.99

If you long to explore creative, two-way communication with the amazing God of the universe… If you would love the familiar, well-read Scriptures to seem fresh and new again… this book is for you. Discover the link between prayer and biblical meditation with popular *Closer to God* contributor Sheila Pritchard. This is a practical book with many 'try it' suggestions.

B format, 128pp

Understanding the Bible

John Stott   ISBN 1 85999 640 X   £6.99

A newly revised edition of a widely-acclaimed classic bestseller. Outstanding Christian teacher and author John Stott examines the cultural, social, geographical and historical background of the Bible, outlining the story and explaining the message. This new edition features focus questions at the beginning of each chapter, new up-to-date maps, and a full index.

B format, 214pp